Everyday Microwave Cooking for Everyday Cooks

Dual Power Cookbook

TOSHIBA

A Message from Toshiba

Welcome to the exciting world of microwave cookery! This is the most beneficial and fun appliance you will own. It will assist you in so many areas that you'll wonder how you used to get through the day without it!

This book has one purpose: **to teach you to cook with microwave energy.** Therefore, you'll find a lot of general rules and theory throughout its pages. These are easy to learn. In fact, we are confident that all of your favorite recipes can become "microwave" recipes.

Honesty and common sense were used to evaluate our recommended recipes and methods. Before including the information, we asked ourselves "would we make this recipe?" or "is this an appropriate food for the microwave oven?" We hope you will fully utilize our suggestions and use this as your guide to microwave cookery.

A microwave oven is a very practical appliance. Use it not only by itself, but in conjunction with the other appliances in your kitchen to maximize its value to you. Be sure to read our chapter "Getting the Most Out of Your Microwave Oven."

Enough said. Turn the page and start reading so you can start cooking! In your new Toshiba Microwave Oven, that is. Thank you for selecting ours!

Acknowledgements

Thanks to the following home economists for their assistance in this cookbook:

Recipe Development: WENDE SOLISH and JEAN E. CAREY
Recipe Testing: DENISE LABUDA, CATHY PHIPPS, DANA FEASTER, DEBBIE GRICE

Table of Contents

Precautions To Avoid Possible Exposure To Excessive Microwave Energy

(a) Do not attempt to operate this oven with the door open since open-door operation can result in harmful exposure to microwave energy. It is important not to defeat or tamper with the safety interlocks.

(b) Do not place any object between the oven front face and the door or allow soil or cleaner residue to accumulate on sealing surfaces.

(c) Do not operate the oven if it is damaged. It is particularly important that the oven door close properly and that there is no damage to the:
(1) door (bent)
(2) hinges and latches (broken or loosened)
(3) door seals and sealing surfaces.

(d) The oven should not be adjusted or repaired by anyone except properly qualified service personnel.

TOSHIBA AMERICA, INC.

CORPORATE HEAD QUARTERS:
82 Totowa Road, Wayne, New Jersey 07470 Phone(201)628-8000
REGIONAL SALES OFFICES:
EAST :82 Totowa Road, Wayne, New Jersey 07470 Phone(201)628-8000
MIDWEST :2900 Mac Arthur Boulevard, Northbrook. Illinois 60062 Phone(312)564-1200
SOUTHWEST:3225 East Carpenter Freeway, Irving, Texas 75062 Phone(214)438-8223
WEST :19500 South Vsrmont avenue Torrance, California 90502 Phone(213)770-3300

TOSHIBA OF CANADA LTD.

Head Office: 3680 Victoria Park Avenue. Willowdale Ontario Phone(416)499-5555
Montreal Branch Office: 1643 North Service Road. Trans-Canada Highway, Dorval, Quebec Phone(514)683-8900
Vancouver Branch Office: 3657 Wayburne Drive, Burnaby, British Columbia Phone(604)291-2966
Calgary Branch Office: 115 28TH Street S.E. Calgary, Alberta Phone(403)273-6906

TOSHIBA HAWAII, INC.

Head Office: 327 Kamakee Street, Honolulu, Hawaii 96814 Phone(808)521-5377

Understanding this Cookbook

A Brief Explanation of How this book is Organized will Aid in its Use as a Quick Reference Guide.

Introduction to Microwave Cooking: The Basics

The first section of this book covers some very basic information on cooking with microwave energy. Please read it carefully as this knowledge will help you to understand the basic principles you will be using throughout the book.

Chapter Introductions

Each chapter covers the correct method for preparing the foods within it. Familiarize yourself with the general rules and microwave oven methods. Before you know it these general rules will become automatic and you'll refer to this book less and less. At least that's our hope! Except to make one of our great recipes.

Wattage Output Levels

Your oven is equipped with two or more cooking speeds. Recipes throughout this book utilize two cooking speeds. They are: Full Power or Medium/Defrost. Use the proper power level given in the recipe for best results. Remember, the times are approximate and each time you prepare a recipe record your actual cooking time in the space provided. Most foods can be cooked on full power but they may require more attention while cooking. The main reason for slowing the cooking down is to gain the control needed to achieve the desired cooking results with each food item.

Recipes

Every recipe in this book contains the following information at the top for quick reference:
Total Cooking Time
Number of Servings
Appropriate Cooking Utensil

The proper power level is given as; **HIGH** (full power) or **MED/DEF**.
Select the proper power level for accurate cooking results. Some recipes will have a symbol placed in the marginbeside the title. These symbols are listed below.

QUICK TO PREPARE

REHEATS EASILY

EASILY PREPARED BY CHILDREN

Adapting Your Favorite Recipes to the Microwave Oven

One of the main goals of this book is to enable you to prepare your everyday dishes in the microwave oven. To do this, evaluate the recipe as to the type of food. (Example: casserole, meat, vegetable, etc.) Turn to that chapter. Each chapter contains instructions as to power levels, cooking times, internal doneness temperatures, and special tips for that type of food. Adapt your recipe by following these general instructions. May we suggest, each time you try a new recipe in the microwave oven, that your record the power level and cooking time on the recipe.

Adapting Other Microwave Recipes to Your Toshiba Microwave Oven

If the recipe is written for full power, check the cookbook for the wattage output used to obtain the cooking times. If the output power is the same as your oven, then the times should be correct. The wattage output of your oven is found in accompanying owners guide manual.

Introduction To Microwave Cooking: The Basics

Microwave Energy

Microwaves are a perfect cooking medium. They allow cool, fast, economical and carefree preparation of meals. A brief explanation of microwave principles will help you understand how heat is generated within the food rather than from an outside source such as gas flame or electric element.

What is a Microwave? A microwave is an electromagnetic wave similar to a light wave with the following characteristics:
1. The ability to be reflected
2. The ability to transmit
3. The ability to be absorbed

These basic characteristics of a microwave are important in the designs of the microwave oven. The object of the oven is to direct the microwaves to be food being cooked. **Metal reflects microwaves** so the metal oven walls reflect the microwaves continually into the oven cavity. Proper utensils for microwave cooking are; **glass, plastic, paper, ceramic,** etc. **These materials are transmitted** by the microwave which means it has no effect on them. **Food items** are made of molecules which will **absorb** microwave energy.

How Do Microwaves Cause Heat Within The Food? Microwaves produced by your oven are moving 2½ billion cycles a second. This movement causes the molecules within the food to rotate 180 degrees 2½ billion times a second. As a result, the molecules are vibrating next to each other causing friction which produces heat. Microwaves cook food from the outside-in, because as the wave penetrates the food, it loses half of its energy for each ¾ inch of food it penetrates. In general, microwaves produce "moist" rather than "dry" heat. (Conventional ovens cook with "dry" heat and conduction rather than penetration).

New Cooking Techniques

As with any new appliance, there are a few basics you must learn to get the full benefit from that appliance. The microwave oven is no exception, so read this next section carefully!

Timing

Learning how long to cook foods is easy when you become familiar with the various things that affect the cooking time. Generally, these are:

1. **Amount of food:** The amount of food placed in a microwave oven has a direct effect on the amount of time it will take to cook it. As an example, one potato will absorb all of the energy in the oven and cook in about 5 minutes. Two potatoes will have to split the microwave energy between them thus taking a longer time.

2. **Wattage Output: One of the most important factors in cooking time is the wattage output of your oven.** Each microwave oven manufactured will cook a little differently and is unique both in its cooking pattern and its speed. **Therefore, consider all recommended cooking times whether given in charts or recipes as approximate.** The first time you cook an item, set the time for less than the recommended time. Check and if necessary, add all or part of the remaining time. If you write the actual time in the cookbook, next time you'll know exactly how long to set the timer!

   TIP: To adjust the cooking time when doubling recipes or amounts use 1½ times the original time. Check to see if the food is done, if not, give it a little more time until it tests done. It is always better to underset the time than to overcook the food.

Original Time	Double Recipe	Additional Time
10 minutes	10 min x 1½ = 15 min.	Only if Necessary

3. **Density:** The density of the food determines how easily the microwave can penetrate and therefore, how quickly it will cook. The more porous the food, the faster it will cook. For example; bread is more porous than steak and will heat in a matter of seconds. The steak will require 3 to 4 minutes.
4. **Starting temperature:** Just as with a conventional range the colder the starting temperature of food, the longer it will take to cook. A food item taken straight from the refrigerator will take a few minutes longer to cook than a food that is room temperature when put into the microwave oven.
5. **Arrangement of Food on Oven Tray:** Arrange the food on the oven tray as shown below for best cooking results. Do not place one item in center and others around it. The outside will attract the microwave energy first and actually keep the one in the center from being cooked.

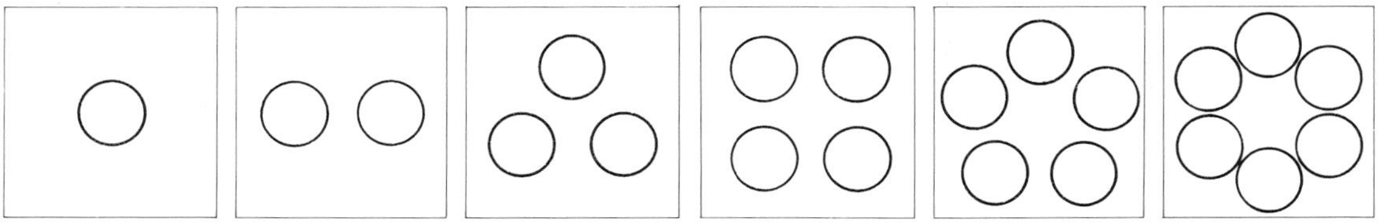

1 item **2 items** **3 items** **4 items** **5 items** **6 items**

TIP: If the food is uneven in shape, place the smaller end toward the center of the oven.

6. **Shaping Food Properly:** Microwaves cook from the outside in, so keeping this in mind will help you select the proper shape for a food. Example: a meatloaf can be shaped several ways and each shape will change the time and the cooking results.

SHAPE	TIME	RESULTS
Loaf taller in center	15—18 min.	Could over-cook on edges before the center is done.
Ring Shape	12—15 min.	No center to cook so will be uniformly cooked.
Small Loaves	12 min.	If shaped no more than 2 inches thick, will be a time saver over full size loaf. Try round rather than loaf shapes.

Most foods can be cooked in a variety of dishes. In each recipe and chapter heading we have suggested the best shaped dish for each food. Use these as guidelines to assure even cooking.

Cooking Terms

Stirring or Turning: Just as some foods require stirring when cooked conventionally, they may also require stirring or turning in the microwave oven.
What does stirring accomplish? Stirring brings the food from the center of the dish, which cooks more slowly, to the outside of the dish where it will heat more quickly.
What does the turning accomplish? Some foods cannot be stirred such as cake, meatloaf, etc. By turning the dish, the food is put into a different cooking pattern. This should aid in even cooking.

TIP: The appearance of the food as it cooks is your guide to how evenly it is cooking. If it is cooking evenly, leave it alone. If not, then turning or stirring will help equally distribute the heat in the food.

Shielding: Shielding is the use of **small** pieces of aluminum foil to reflect the microwaves away from an area that is cooking too quickly. An example is a turkey. The legs and wings may cook more quickly than the breast. By placing a small piece of foil over the leg or wing, the microwaves cannot cook them any further. Caution should be taken when placing the foil in the oven. Be sure it is no closer than 1 inch from the ovens walls.

Standing Time: Microwave energy creates heat within the food. As a result, the food continues to cook for a few minutes after being removed from the oven. This is called "carryover cooking." Keep this in mind and undercook, then allow the food to stand for a few minutes before serving. This standing time also allows the heat to distribute evenly throughout the entire dish.

General Rules

1. Always allow a standing time before serving.
2. Cook one recipe at a time rather than several dishes at once.
   Each recipe will cook faster alone. Each item may also vary in density and require different power levels. (See menu planning section for proper cooking order of recipe).
3. Arrange the food properly in the dish or on oven tray.
4. Set the timer for less than the total cooking time until you become familiar with how much time various foods require.
5. Record the cooking time and power level on any recipes you try for future reference.

Proper Utensils for Proper Cooking Result

Just as the shape of the food can assure even cooking, the shape of the dish will also help. Use the guide below for selecting the proper utensil.

SHAPE	COOKING RESULTS
Ring Shape	Excellent — microwaves can enter from both outside and center of dish. Food will cook faster and very evenly.
Round	Very Good — eliminates any corners which may cook faster than center.
Covered Dishes	Very Good — cover will help hold heat in food so the center will heat more quickly.
Square	Good — corners may cook before the center. Proper arrangement of food is essential. May need to slow down the cooking speed to assure food is done in center and edges at the same time.
Oblong	Good — puts a lot of food in center which cooks slower. Care must be taken in placement of food in dish and cooking speed to assure food being done in center and edges at same time.

TIP: Before you put the recipe in a dish, think about the way microwaves cook that food and how quickly you want it to cook. Then select the proper shape utensil.

Special Microwave Cooking Accessories

There are several accessories available today designed to help you get proper cooking results with a microwave oven. A list is given and their proper uses to guide you in the purchase of these special accessories.

Browning Dish — A specially designed dish which when pre-heated in a microwave oven will sear meats to give them a brown appearance. The bottom of this dish is coated with a special material which absorbs microwave energy and then gets extremely hot. It is this hot area which is searing the food while the microwaves cook the food. For full instructions, refer to the book packed with the browning dish.

Roasting Rack – This is a plastic rack which is designed to hold a roast up out of the juice that accumulates around it. The result is more even cooking of the meat. When not used, the meat has a tendency to cook more in the area submerged in the juices.

Microwave Oven Thermometer – This thermometer is designed for use in a microwave oven. Even though it is metal it can stay in the microwave oven during the entire cooking time. **Do not use a conventional meat or candy thermometer in a microwave oven.** They are not designed to hold up under microwave energy.

Tube, Ring or Bundt Dishes – Several companies now offer plastic or ceramic dishes in these shapes. These are useful with recipes that should be cooked in a ring shape.

Plastic Cupcake Pan – Plastic dish used for baking cupcakes, muffins etc. It places the cupcakes in the proper arrangement for microwave cooking.

How to Defrost Foods

Learning the proper defrosting methods will make defrosting a breeze. Your microwave oven uses its reduced cooking power to defrost foods by heating the ice crystals just enough to dissolve them but not cook the food. Once again, the same things that affect how quickly a food will heat will also affect how quickly a food will defrost. A loaf of bread will defrost very quickly, a roast will require more time, etc.

Standing Time: One secret to defrosting is allowing the food to stand after the completion of the defrosting time. This is called "standing time" and will allow the heat to evenly distribute throughout the food, dissolving the icy center. Addition of more microwave energy could cause the outside to start cooking.

Refer to the Defrosting chart in the back of the book for proper defrosting times.

NOTE: The temperature in freezers vary, so the times given in the chart may require lengthening if you own a separate freezer. A good rule is to set for suggested time, allow the standing time, then add additional time if necessary.

How to Reheat Food

Reheated foods need only to be heated to a temperature comfortable to the palate. Thus, these foods needn't be heated as hot as their original cooking temperature. Some general rules to follow:

1. Store leftovers in a suitable microwave oven utensil to eliminate extra dishes.
2. Cover with either a lid or pleated plastic wrap.
3. When reheating several different types of food on one plate, place the large, more dense items to the outer edges and smaller or more porous items toward the center. Then, everything will be heated through and hot at the same time.
4. Heat for suggested time and at suggested power level given on reheating chart, page 174.
5. Allow standing time for heat to be evenly distributed throughout food.

Appetizers & Snacks

Appetizers and snacks can always be ready in a snap even when unexpected company arrives. With the help of your microwave oven, most recipes can be cooked and served in the same dish. Reheating a second serving is fast. It's fun to let your guest heat his own and you can show off your new microwave oven.

As a General Rule

- Cook covered if preparing a dip or appetizer in a sauce recipe.
- Cook uncovered if the recipe calls for bread or cracker type ingredients, unless heating a large quantity, then cover loosely with wax paper. Cook directly on serving platter.
- A doily placed on serving platter will help absorb moisture when heating crackers topped with cheese, etc.
- When reheating use power level HIGH.
- Remember that the more items you are heating the longer it will take. Appetizers heat very quickly so watch them carefully.

Microwave Method

Generally, preparing appetizers is a matter of heating a mixture of foods, dips or assorted toppings on crackers. The main thing to consider is how long to heat the item you want to serve. Follow the steps below and use the Appetizer Heating Chart as a guide in heating times for your favorite recipes.

1. Prepare recipe as directed and heat in microwave oven according to chart.
2. When heating individual items, place them in a circle to insure even heating.

APPETIZER HEATING CHART

Type of Appetizer	Amount	Power Level	Heating Time
Hot Dip	2 cups	HIGH	2 to 3 min.
Meat in Sauce	4 cups	HIGH	8 to 10 min.
Canapes			
Cheese	12	HIGH	2 min.
Meat	12	HIGH	3 min.

15
Appetizers & Snacks

Island Beef Skewers

TOTAL COOKING TIME: 20 minutes
Makes 24 appetizers
13 x 9-inch glass baking dish

1 pound flank steak, sliced diagonally, then into 1-inch pieces
1 jar (10-ounces) apricot pineapple jam
1 bottle (8-ounces) teriyaki marinade
1 can (20-ounces) pineapple chunks, well drained
1 large green pepper, cut into 1-inch chunks
24 6-inch wooden skewers
2 tablespoons sesame seeds

In glass baking dish, combine teriyaki marinade, apricot pineapple jam and flank steak pieces. Let sit for at least 45 minutes. Ten minutes before skewering, add pineapple and green pepper to marinade. On each skewer slide on beef, pineapple, and green pepper. Repeat and end with beef. Drain excess marinade out of dish. In same dish place 12 filled skewers. Sprinkle with half of sesame seeds. Cook on **HIGH** for 10 minutes, stopping midway to drain any accumulated liquid. Repeat with remaining skewers.

My cooking time: ☐

Cheesy Gherkin Ham Rollups

TOTAL COOKING TIME: 3 minutes
Makes 14 appetizers
9-inch square glass baking dish

1 bottle (12-ounces) sweet gherkins, halved lengthwise
1 package (8-ounces) sliced ham, cut in halves
1 cup grated Cheddar cheese
Toothpicks

Place one halved sweet gherkin lengthwise onto each piece of ham. Sprinkle with cheese. Roll up ham slice and secure with wooden pick. Place in glass baking dish. Cover; cook on **HIGH** for 2½ minutes or until cheese is melted.

My cooking time: ☐

Bacon Sticks

TOTAL COOKING TIME: 10 minutes
Makes 10 appetizers
11 x 9-inch glass baking dish

10 pencil thin cheese flavored bread sticks
5 slices lean bacon

Slice bacon in half lengthwise, and wrap each half around breadstick, spiral fashion. Line glass baking dish with 3 thicknesses of paper towel. Place bacon sticks on top; cover with another paper towel to avoid spattering. Cook on **HIGH** for 9 to 10 minutes, or until crisp.

My cooking time: ☐

Scampi

TOTAL COOKING TIME: 5 minutes
Serves 4
1½-quart glass casserole dish

¼ cup butter
4 large garlic cloves, finely diced
1 tablespoon chopped parsley
1 tablespoon lemon juice
2 teaspoons grated Parmesan cheese
½ pound medium shrimp, shelled and deveined

In glass casserole, cook butter on **HIGH** for 1½ minutes or until melted. Add garlic; cook on **HIGH** for 1½ minutes or until butter is bubbly. Mix in Parmesan cheese, parsley, lemon juice and shrimp. Cook on **HIGH** for 2 minutes or until shrimp is cooked.

My cooking time: ☐

Appetizers & Snacks

Glazed Halibut

TOTAL COOKING TIME: 10 minutes
Serves 4
11 x 9-inch glass baking dish
1 pint glass bowl

4 halibut steaks (about 2 pounds)
2 teaspoons gelatin powder
½ cup mayonnaise
1 tablespoon chili sauce or catsup
½ teaspoon dill weed
1 hard cooked egg, shredded

In glass baking dish, cook halibut on **HIGH** for 7 to 9 minutes, or until fish flakes with a fork, turning dish once during cooking. Drain and reserve accumulated liquid. Remove any skin and bone. Place on serving dish. In glass bowl, combine fish liquid and gelatin powder. Cook on **HIGH** for 1 minute. Add mayonnaise and chili sauce or catsup. Stir well. Pour evenly over fish. Chill to gel. Garnish with shredded egg.

My cooking time: ☐

Polynesian Meatballs

TOTAL COOKING TIME: 16 minutes
Makes 30 meatballs
3-quart covered glass casserole dish

1 pound lean ground beef
1 medium onion, diced
⅛ teaspoon ground ginger
½ cup bread crumbs
1 egg, slightly beaten
2 cans (10½-ounces each) condensed tomato soup
½ cup packed brown sugar
1 can (20-ounces) pineapple chunks, well drained
1 teaspoon salt

Mix together ground beef, half of diced onion, ground ginger, bread crumbs and slightly beaten egg. Shape into walnut size meatballs. Place meatballs into 3-quart glass casserole. Cover, partially cook on **HIGH** for 4 minutes, stirring once during cooking. Meanwhile, in large mixing bowl, mix together condensed tomato soup, brown sugar, remaining onion and pineapple chunks, and add to partially cooked meatballs. Coat well, being careful not to break up meatballs. Cover; cook on **HIGH** for 12 minutes stirring twice during cooking.

My cooking time: ☐

Crab Canapes

TOTAL COOKING TIME: 2 minutes
Makes 20 appetizers
13 x 9-inch glass baking dish or serving platter

1 can (6½-ounces) crab meat
½ cup mayonnaise
¼ cup grated Cheddar cheese
2 tablespoons finely diced onion
1 tablespoon parsley flakes
1 teaspoon white horseradish
1 teaspoon tomato catsup
½ teaspoon Worcestershire sauce
Salt to taste
20 Melba crackers or toasted bread squares

In glass mixing bowl, combine all ingredients, except Melba crackers or toasted bread squares. Mix well. Heap slightly less than a tablespoon of mixture onto each cracker or bread square. Place on glass tray lined with paper towel or doily. Cover; cook on **HIGH** for 1½ minutes or until cheese is melted. Garnish as desired.

My cooking time: ☐

◄ *Top to bottom: Glazed Halibut and Crab Canapes.*

Escargot

TOTAL COOKING TIME: 4 minutes
Makes 18 appetizers
9-inch glass baking dish

½ cup butter
1 tablespoon lemon juice
4 cloves garlic, diced or pressed
2 tablespoons Parmesan cheese
1 can (4½-ounces) snails
French bread

In glass baking dish, cook butter on **HIGH** for 1¼ minutes or until melted. Add cheese, garlic and lemon juice. Mix well. Add snails, cover; cook on **HIGH** for 2 minutes or until hot. Tuck snails into individual escargot shells if desired. Serve with French bread.

My cooking time: ☐

Stuffed Mushrooms

TOTAL COOKING TIME: 7 minutes
Makes 25 to 30 appetizers
1-quart glass casserole
9-inch round glass baking dish

½ pound medium size mushrooms
2 tablespoons butter
½ cup finely chopped green onion
1 hard cooked egg, finely chopped
1 tablespoon parsley flakes

Clean mushrooms and snap stems from caps. Dice stems and put caps aside. In glass casserole, cook butter on **HIGH** for 1¼ minutes or until melted. Add diced stems and onion. Cook on **HIGH** for 2 minutes or until both are tender. Drain any liquid accumulated. Mix in finely chopped egg and parsley flakes. In glass baking dish, cover and cook mushroom caps, on **HIGH** for 2 to 3 minutes or until tender. Generously stuff each cooked mushroom cap with diced mixture. To reheat, cook covered on **HIGH** for 2 minutes. Serve hot.

My cooking time: ☐

Crispy Oriental Chicken Wings

TOTAL COOKING TIME: 20 minutes
Makes about 24 appetizers
13 x 9-inch glass baking dish

1½ pounds chicken wings, disjointed
1 medium egg
½ cup soy sauce
2 tablespoons garlic powder
¼ teaspoon ginger powder
1 medium onion finely diced
2 cups finely crushed corn flakes

Mix together egg, soy sauce, garlic powder and ginger powder. Set aside. On wax paper, mix together crushed corn flakes and diced onion. Dip each wing in soy sauce mixture, then roll in corn flakes and onion. In glass baking dish, cover and cook wings, on **HIGH** for 20 minutes or until cooked. Remove covering half way through cooking.

My cooking time: ☐

Sour Cream'n Sausages

TOTAL COOKING TIME: 8 minutes
Makes 48 appetizers
1½-quart glass casserole dish

1 can (10½-ounces) condensed cream of celery soup
1 cup sour cream
¼ cup prepared mustard
1 pound cocktail weiner sausages
Toothpicks

In glass casserole, mix together soup, sour cream and mustard. Stir in weiners. Cover; cook on **HIGH** for 8 minutes or until hot, stirring once during cooking. Serve with toothpicks.

My cooking time: ☐

Appetizers & Snacks

Hot Mexican Bean Dip

TOTAL COOKING TIME: 5 minutes
Makes about 4 cups
1-quart glass serving bowl

1 can (16-ounces) refried beans
1 jar (8-ounces) pasteurized processed cheese spread
1 can (4-ounces) diced green chiles
1 large tomato, diced
Salsa to taste
Corn chips

In glass serving bowl, cook all ingredients except corn chips on **MED/DEF** for 5 minutes or until cheese is melted. Stir during cooking. Serve hot with corn chips.

My cooking time: ______

TIP: If salsa is not available, use chili powder to taste.

Spicy Sugared Nuts

TOTAL COOKING TIME: 25 minutes
Makes 2 cups
1-quart glass mixing bowl
13 x 9-inch glass baking dish

1 cup packed brown sugar
¼ cup orange juice
1 tablespoon butter
1 teaspoon cinnamon
¼ teaspoon ground cloves
¼ teaspoon nutmeg
2 cup unsalted nuts

In glass mixing bowl, combine all ingredients except nuts. Cook on **HIGH** for 5 minutes or until syrupy, stirring once during cooking. Mix nuts into syrup mixture, stirring well to coat. In glass baking dish, lined with oiled wax paper, evenly spread out nuts. Cook on **MED/DEF** for 20 minutes or until no longer sticky; stir well every 5 minutes.

My cooking time: ______

Bridge Mix

TOTAL COOKING TIME: 5 minutes
Makes 5 cups
1½-quart glass casserole dish

1 cup bite size cheese crackers
1 cup oyster crackers
1 cup thin pretzel sticks
1 cup bite size shredded bran squares
1 package (2½-ounces) salted cashew nuts
4 tablespoons melted butter
¼ cup grated Parmesan cheese
1 tablespoon soy sauce
1 teaspoon Italian seasoning
Salt to taste

In glass casserole, combine crackers, cereal, pretzels and nuts. In separate small mixing bowl, stir together melted butter, cheese, soy sauce and Italian seasoning. Pour liquid mixture over dry mixture. Stir well to coat. Cook on **HIGH** for 5 minutes or until mixture is dry, stirring every minute.

My cooking time: ______

Note: Because of the delicate nature of this recipe, it is essential to stir every minute to avoid burning in spots.

Quesadillas

TOTAL COOKING TIME: 4 minutes
Serves 4
13 x 9-inch glass baking dish

4 flour tortillas
1 cup shredded Cheddar or Jack cheese
4 teaspoons diced onion
4 teaspoons diced green chiles
1 small tomato, diced

Place an even amount of cheese, onion, chiles and tomato onto each tortilla. Fold tortilla over once. Place in baking dish and cook on **MED/DEF** for 4 minutes or until cheese is melted. Serve hot.

My cooking time: ☐

TIP: Be creative with Quesadilla fillings. You may add mushrooms, meat or any cooked vegatables you desire, or you may omit the onion, chiles or tomato.

Sloppy Joes

TOTAL COOKING TIME: 11 minutes
Serves 4
1½-quart glass casserole dish
13 x 9-inch glass dish

1 pound lean ground beef
4 slices uncooked bacon, diced
1 small green pepper, finely diced
1 small onion, diced
1 can (15-ounces) chili beans
1 can (8-ounces) tomato sauce
1 tablespoon chili powder
1 teaspoon garlic powder
1 teaspoon salt
4 hamburger buns
½ cup grated Cheddar cheese

In glass casserole, combine ground beef, diced bacon, green pepper, and onion. Mix well. Cook on **HIGH** for 6 minutes or until meat is no longer pink, stirring once during cooking. Drain. Add remaining ingredients except hamburger buns and cheese. Mix well. In glass dish place open hamburger buns and heap each half with an equal amount of beef mixture. Sprinkle with grated cheese. Cover; cook on **HIGH** for 4 to 5 minutes or until cheese is melted.

My cooking time: ☐

Ramaki

TOTAL COOKING TIME: 9 minutes
Makes about 27 appetizers
1-quart glass baking dish

9 slices bacon cut in thirds
1 can (5-ounces) water chestnuts
Teriyaki marinade

Wrap each bacon piece around one water chestnut and secure with toothpick. Place in Teriyaki marinade for at least 30 minutes. Drain excess marinade and place ramaki in glass baking dish lined with paper towel. Cook on **HIGH** for about 9 minutes or until bacon is crisp.

My cooking time: ☐

TIP: Water chestnuts can be replaced with smoked oysters or pineapple chunks.

Beverages

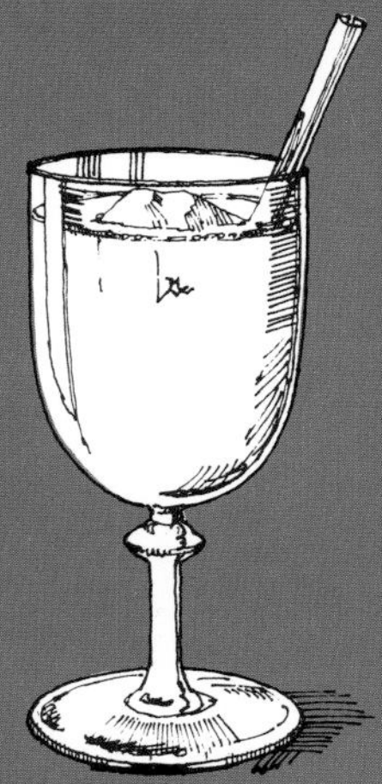

Imagine a cup of coffee in 1 minute or hot mulled punch heated right in the punch bowl. These conveniences are possible when cooking with microwave energy. Beverages like coffee and tea can be reheated to fresh perked or brewed flavor right in the mug.

As a General Rule

- When heating individual cups there is no need to cover.
- When heating large quantities, it will take less time if the container is covered.
- Heat on power level HIGH unless the beverage contains milk, then use power level MED/DEF.
- Heat beverages in glass, ceramic, pottery or plastic mugs or pitchers. (Be sure there is no metallic trim.) Heating large quantities in a pitcher makes it easy to serve and leaves fewer dirty dishes.
- To allow flavors to blend in a spicy punch, heat to a boiling point and let simmer a few minutes on a lower power level before serving.

Microwave Method

Heating beverages is a simple matter of bringing the liquid to a serving temperature. A serving temperature is a matter of personal taste. We have based our heating chart on a serving temperature of 160°F. For a lower serving temperature, reduce the amount of cooking time.

1. Place beverage in microwave oven and set for power level and time suggested on Beverage Heating Chart.
2. Stir before serving.

BEVERAGE HEATING CHART

Amount	Time on *HIGH	Time on **MED/DEF
	Water Base	Milk Base
1 cup	2 min.	2½ min.
2 cups	3—4 min.	5 min.
1 quart	6—7 min.	7—8 min.
2 quarts	10—12 min.	4—6 min.

*Times based on room temperature liquid.
**Times based on refrigerated temperature liquid.

Beverages

Hot Mulled Cider

TOTAL COOKING TIME: 8 minutes
Makes 1 quart
2-quart glass bowl

1 quart apple cider
4 cinnamon sticks
1 tablespoon allspice
16 whole cloves
1 tablespoon honey
1 orange, sliced
1 lemon, sliced

In glass bowl, combine all ingredients. Cook on **HIGH** for 8 minutes or until boiling. Strain into mugs.

My cooking time: ☐

Apple Nog

TOTAL COOKING TIME: 6-7 minutes
Serves 4
2-quart glass bowl

2 eggs, lightly beaten
¼ cup sugar
1 teaspoon cinnamon
Dash nutmeg
1 cup apple juice
3 cups milk
4 cinnamon sticks

In glass bowl, combine all ingredients except milk and cinnamon sticks. Gradually stir in milk. Cover; cook on **HIGH** for 6 to 7 minutes or just until mixture begins to boil; stirring twice during cooking. Pour into mugs and serve with a cinnamon stick in each mug.

My cooking time: ☐

Hot Buttered Rum

TOTAL COOKING TIME: 5 minutes
Serves 4
2-quart glass bowl

1 can (16-ounces) evaporated milk
1 cup molasses
½ cup butter, melted
1 teaspoon vanilla
1 teaspoon cinnamon
4 jiggers dark rum

In glass bowl, combine milk, molasses and butter. Stir well. Cover; cook on **HIGH** for 5 minutes or until bubbling, stir once during cooking.Stir in vanilla, cinnamon and rum. Serve hot in mugs.

My cooking time: ☐

Mocha Coffee

TOTAL COOKING TIME: 2 minutes
Serves 1
8-ounce coffee mug

¾ cup strong black coffee
1 teaspoon instant cocoa
½ jigger coffee liquer
½ jigger chocolate liqueur
Whipped cream

In serving mug, cook coffee and cocoa on **HIGH** for 2 minutes or until very hot. Add liqueur. Top with whipped cream.

My cooking time: ☐

Spiced Coffee

TOTAL COOKING TIME: 2 minutes
Serves 1
8-ounce coffee mug

¾ cup strong black coffee
1 teaspoon milk
2 teaspoon sugar
1 stick cinnamon
Dash nutmeg
Whipped cream

In serving mug, cook coffee on **HIGH** for 2 minutes or until very hot. Add milk, sugar and nutmeg. Top with whipped cream and serve with cinnamon stick.

My cooking time: ☐

Irish Coffee

TOTAL COOKING TIME: 2 minutes
Serves 1
8-ounce coffee mug

¾ cup strong black coffee
1 jigger Irish whiskey
Whipped cream

In serving mug, cook coffee on **HIGH** for 2 minutes, or until very hot. Stir in sugar and whiskey. Top with whipped cream.

My cooking time: ☐

Brandied Almond Coffee

TOTAL COOKING TIME: 2 minutes
Serves 1
8-ounce coffee mug

¾ cup strong black coffee
1 jigger Creme de Almond
½ jigger Brandy
Whipped cream

In serving mug, cook coffee on **HIGH** for 2 minutes or until very hot. Add Creme de Almond and Brandy. Top with whipped cream.

My cooking time: ☐

Mocha Mint Coffee

TOTAL COOKING TIME: 2 minutes
Serves 1
8-ounce coffee mug

¾ cup strong black coffee
1 teaspoon instant hot cocoa
1 jigger Creme de Cacao
½ jigger Creme de Menthe
Whipped cream

In serving mug, cook coffee and cocoa on **HIGH** for 2 minutes or until very hot. Add liqueurs. Top with whipped cream.

My cooking time: ☐

Mexican Coffee

TOTAL COOKING TIME: 2 minutes
Serves 1
8-ounce coffee mug

¾ cup strong black coffee
¼ cup milk or cream
1 jigger Kahlua
Whipped cream

In serving mug, cook coffee and cream on **HIGH** for 2 minutes or until very hot. Add Kahlua. Top with whipped cream.

My cooking time: ☐

Chateau Spiced Burgundy

TOTAL COOKING TIME: 8 minutes
Serves 2
2-quart glass bowl

1 bottle (25.4-ounces) Burgundy
1 cup sugar
1 orange, sliced
½ teaspoon cloves
2 sticks cinnamon
2 cups water

In glass bowl, combine all ingredients except Burgundy. Cook on **HIGH** for 8 minutes, or until boiling. Strain into punch bowl, add Burgundy. Serve warm.

My cooking time: ☐

Soups & Casseroles

Hearty, old fashioned soups and casseroles lend themselves beautifully to the microwave oven. The vegetables used retain their beautiful color and fresh flavor because the cooking time is much shorter than when cooked conventionally. Cook the soup right in the tureen or serving bowl and it's ready to go to the table.

As a General Rule: Soups

- Cook covered in heat proof glass dish.
- Cook in serving bowl to save dishes.
- If adding vegetables or pasta to a soup recipe add during last half of cooking time.

Microwave Method: Soups

Soups generally require long slow cooking to fully develop the flavor. Our method is given below:

1. Follow recipe and prepare ingredients as directed.
2. Place in large bowl. Cover and cook on power level HIGH for 10 minutes to bring to a boil.
3. Reduce power level to MED/DEF and cook for total of 1/2 the conventional cooking time.
4. Add vegetables during last half of microwave cooking time.

As a General Rule: Casseroles

- Cook in a glass heat proof dish.
- Cook covered.
- Stir or turn once during cooking time for fastest heating.
- If in deep large container heat for longer time than if using a shallow dish.
- If cheese is called for as topping, add only during last few minutes of cooking time.
- If browned crust is desired on top, sprinkle with a mixture of cheese and bread crumbs or wheat germ. If further browning is desired, put under conventional broiler for a few minutes.

Microwave Method: Casseroles

Most casseroles are a combination of precooked foods, thus they need only to be heated to combine flavors and bring to a serving temperature. To prepare your favorite recipe, cook as follows:

1. Cook ingredients as directed and assemble casserole in a glass dish, (Most ingredients can be cooked in the microwave oven)
2. Cover and cook on HIGH until hot and bubbly. A 1½-quart casserole will take approximately 12–15 minutes. The larger the amount, the longer the cooking time.

Enchilada Pie

TOTAL COOKING TIME: 14 minutes
Serves 4
2-quart covered glass casserole

1 pound lean ground beef
2 tablespoons onion
1½ cups grated Cheddar cheese, divided
1 can (4-ounces) diced green chiles
1 can (6-ounces) tomatoes, chopped
½ package (9½-ounces) corn chips
1 teaspoon hot chili powder
1 cup shredded lettuce
1 large tomato, sliced
Salt to taste

In glass casserole, cook ground beef and onion on **HIGH** for 5 minutes or until beef is no longer pink. Drain. Stir in 1 cup cheese, chiles, canned tomatoes, and corn chips. Cover; cook on **HIGH** for 6 minutes or until hot. Sprinkle remaining ½ cup cheese on top. Continue cooking on **HIGH** for 3 minutes or until cheese melts. Garnish with shredded lettuce and sliced tomato.

My cooking time: ______

Tamale Bake

TOTAL COOKING TIME: 15 minutes
Serves 4
2-quart covered glass casserole

1 pound lean ground beef
½ cup chopped onion
½ cup sliced black olives
2 teaspoons chili powder
1 can (16-ounces) tomato sauce, divided
1½ teaspoons salt, divided
1 cup yellow corn meal
1 cup water
¾ cup milk
1 can (4-ounces) diced green chiles
½ cup grated Cheddar cheese

In glass casserole cook ground beef and onion on **HIGH** for 5 minutes or until beef is no longer pink. Stir in olives, chili powder, half of tomato sauce and 1 teaspoon salt. Set aside. In glass mixing bowl, cook corn meal, water, milk, chiles and ½ teaspoon salt on **HIGH** for 3½ minutes or until thick, stirring twice during cooking. Spoon evenly over beef. Spread remaining tomato sauce on top. Sprinkle with cheese. Cover; cook on **HIGH** for 7 minutes or until hot and cheese is melted.

My cooking time: ______

Beef Stroganoff

TOTAL COOKING TIME: 15 minutes
Serves 4
2-quart covered glass casserole

1 pound lean ground beef
1 teaspoon garlic powder
1 medium onion, finely chopped
¼ pound mushrooms, sliced
½ cup red wine
3 tablespoons flour, made into a paste with water
¼ teaspoon pepper
1 teaspoon salt
1 cup sour cream
1 package (8-ounces) flat egg noodles, cooked

In glass casserole, combine beef, onion, and mushrooms. Cook on **HIGH** for 5 minutes or until beef is no longer pink. Add wine, flour paste, salt, and pepper. Stir well. Mix in sour cream. Cover; cook on **HIGH** for 10 minutes or until hot. Serve over hot cooked noodles.

My cooking time: ______

NOTE: You may substitute ¼ cup beef stock plus 1 teaspoon Worcestershire sauce for wine.

SAN
GRATED
100 gr.
Peso netto
Nettogewicht
ITALIENISCHER HARTKÄSE

Soups & Casseroles

Manhattan Clam Chowder

TOTAL COOKING TIME: 25 minutes
Serves 4 to 6
4-quart glass bowl

3 slices uncooked bacon, diced
2 tablespoons butter
⅔ cup celery, diced
⅔ cup onion, diced
2 small potatoes, diced
2 cups tomato juice
1 can (10-ounces) clams, undrained
1 bottle (8-ounces) clam juice
½ cup light cream
3 medium tomatoes, diced
½ teaspoon dill weed
8 frozen clams in the shell

In glass bowl, cook diced bacon on **HIGH** for 3 minutes or until cooked. Add butter, cook on **HIGH** for 1 minute or until butter is melted. Add celery, onion and potatoes. Cover; cook on **HIGH** for 4 minutes or until vegetables are tender, stirring once during cooking. Add remaining ingredients and cook on **HIGH** for 15 to 18 minutes for flavors to combine; stir 3 times during cooking. Add frozen clams during last 5 minutes of cooking. Discard any that have not opened after cooking.

My cooking time: ☐

Onion Gratin Soup

TOTAL COOKING TIME: 36 minutes
Serves 4
4-quart glass bowl

6 tablespoons butter
3 large onions, halved and thinly sliced
2 cans (10½-ounces each) condensed beef consomme
1 cup water
¼ cup dry white wine
1 tablespoon Worcestershire sauce
Salt and pepper to taste
1 loaf French bread, sliced
Parmesan cheeses

In glass bowl, cook butter on **HIGH** for 1½ minutes or until melted. Add onions. Cover; cook on **HIGH** for 20 minutes or until onions are completely soft, stirring twice during cooking. Add consomme, water and wine. Cover; cook on **HIGH** for 10 minutes or until boiling. Pour into 4 individual serving bowls. Place one slice of bread into each bowl and sprinkle with cheese. Cook on **HIGH** for 5 minutes or until cheese is melted. Serve hot with extra French bread.

My cooking time: ☐

Fresh Mushroom Soup

TOTAL COOKING TIME: 18 minutes
Serves 4 to 6
4-quart glass mixing bowl

2 cups chopped fresh mushrooms
2 cups light cream
1 can (10½-ounces) condensed beef consomme
¼ cup dry sherry
2 tablespoons flour
1 tablespoon finely diced onion
1 teaspoon garlic powder
½ teaspoon Worcestershire sauce
¼ teaspoon white pepper
Sour cream

In glass mixing bowl, combine all ingredients, except sour cream. Cook on **HIGH** for 15 to 18 minutes or until thickened. Garnish with dollops of sour cream, if desired.

My cooking time: ☐

◄ *Top to bottom: Manhattan Clan Chowder and Onion Gratin Soup.*

Shrimp 'n Scallop Bisque

TOTAL COOKING TIME: 23 minutes
Serves 4 to 6
2-quart glass mixing bowl
Small glass mixing bowl

- 3 tablespoon butter, divided
- 2 tablespoons flour
- 1½ cups light cream
- ½ cup plus 2 tablespoons Sauterne wine, divided
- ¼ pound fresh mushrooms, sliced
- 2 tablespoons diced onion
- 1 teaspoon garlic powder
- 1 teaspoon salt
- 2 tablespoon lemon juice
- 1 pound scallops
- ½ pound shrimp
- Dash tabasco
- Dash Worcestershire sauce

In large glass mixing bowl, cook 2 tablespoons butter on **HIGH** for 1 minute or until melted. Add flour, light cream and ½ cup wine. Cook on **MEDIUM** for 10 minutes, or until thickend. Set aside. In small mixing bowl, cook remaining 1 tablespoon butter on **HIGH** for 45 seconds, or until melted. Add mushrooms and onions. Cook on **HIGH** for 2 minutes or until onions are transparent. Add mushrooms, onions and remaining ingredients, except wine, to sauce. Cook on **HIGH** for 10 minutes, or until hot. Stir in remaining 2 tablespoons wine. Season to taste with more Tabasco and Worcestershire sauce, if needed.

My cooking time: ______

31
Soups & Casseroles

Hearty Beef Soup

TOTAL COOKING TIME: 33 minutes
Serves 4 to 6
4-quart glass bowl

1 pound lean ground beef
5 cups water
1 can (8-ounces) tomato sauce
2 large tomatoes, chopped
1 envelope (about ¾-ounce) brown gravy mix
1 stalk celery, diced
1 small onion, coarsely chopped
1 carrot, sliced
1 green pepper, coarsely chopped
1 tablespoon Worcestershire sauce
2 teaspoons salt
1 bay leaf
Dash pepper
1 cup uncooked macaroni

In glass bowl, cook beef on **HIGH** for 5 minutes or until no longer pink, stirring once during cooking. Add remaining ingredients, except macaroni. Cover; cook on **HIGH** for 25 to 28 minutes or long enough for flavors to combine, adding macaroni during last 10 minutes of cooking.

My cooking time: ☐

TIP: For a special touch, sprinkle each serving with grated Cheddar cheese.

Corn Chowder

TOTAL COOKING TIME: 20 minutes
Serves 4
2-quart glass mixing bowl

2 tablespoons butter
3 tablespoons chopped onion
2 cups milk
⅓ cup light cream
1 cube beef boullion
1 can (17-ounces) cream style corn
Salt and pepper

In glass bowl, cook butter on **HIGH** for 45 seconds or until melted. Add chopped onion. Cook on **HIGH** for 2 minutes or until onion is transparent. Add milk, cream, and boullion. Cook on **HIGH** for 8 to 10 minutes or until boiling stirring twice during cooking. Add corn and continue cooking on **HIGH** for 7 minutes or until boiling again. Season to taste with salt and pepper.

My cooking time: ☐

Mild Chili Con Carne

TOTAL COOKING TIME: 17 minutes
Serves 4
2-quart glass casserole dish

1 pound lean ground beef
1 small onion, diced
1 medium tomato, diced
½ green pepper, diced
1 can (15-ounces) tomato sauce
1 can (15-ounces) chili beans
1 can (4-ounces) diced green chiles
1 large carrot, grated
1 tablespoon chili powder
1 teaspoon garlic powder
Dash pepper

In glass casserole, cook beef, onion and green pepper on **HIGH** for 5 minutes, or until beef is no longer pink. Add remaining ingredients. Cover; cook on **HIGH** for 12 minutes, or until hot.

My cooking time: ☐

TIP: For a hotter chili, add more chili powder to taste.

◄ *Shrimp'n Scallop Bisque*

Spring Ham Casserole

TOTAL COOKING TIME: 16 minutes
Serves 4
2-quart covered glass casserole dish

2 tablespoon butter
½ cup diced celery
½ cup diced onion
¼ cup chopped green pepper
1 cup light cream
1 tablespoon flour
2 cubes chicken boullion
1 jar (4 -ounces) whole button mushrooms
2 cups diced ham
1 packagé (8-ounces) spaghetti, cooked
¼ cup Parmesan cheese
Salt to taste
Parsley to garnish

In glass casserole, cook butter on **HIGH** for 1 minute or until melted. Add diced celery, onion and green pepper. Cook on **HIGH** for 2 minutes or until onion is transparent. Drain mushroom juice into 1-cup measure and add water to make 1 cup. Add mushroom juice and water, cream, flour and boullion cubes to butter and vegetable mixture. Cook on **HIGH** for 12 to 14 minutes or until thick, stirring twice during cooking. Toss in mushrooms, ham and hot spaghetti. Sprinkle with Parmesan cheese and garnish with parsley.

My cooking time: ________

Beef Chow Mein

TOTAL COOKING TIME: 24 minutes
Serves 4
2-quart glass casserole dish
4-cup glass mixing bowl

1 pound lean ground beef
1 can (10½-ounces) condensed beef consumme
2 tablespoons cornstarch
2 tablespoons soy sauce
1 teaspoon garlic powder
½ teaspoon ground ginger
1 package (6-ounces) frozen Chinese pea pods
½ medium onion, thinly sliced
¼ pound fresh mushrooms, thinly sliced
1 stalk celery, thinly sliced
½ pound fresh bean sprouts
Hot cooked rice

In glass casserole, crumble beef and cook on **HIGH** for 5 minutes or until no longer pink; stir once during cooking. Drain. In glass mixing bowl, combine consumme, cornstarch, soy sauce, garlic powder and ginger. Cook on **HIGH** for 7 minutes, or until mixture thickens; stir twice during cooking. Pour thickened mixture into cooked beef. Add all vegetables except bean sprouts. Cook on **HIGH** for 10 minutes, or until hot, mixing in bean sprouts during last 3 minutes. Serve over hot rice.

My cooking time: ☐

TIP: To avoid lumping, mix just enough consumme into cornstarch to form a thin paste before combining with rest of consumme, and for more even cooking, all vegetables should be cut into uniform sizes.

Lamb Curry

TOTAL COOKING TIME: 17 minutes
Serves 4
2-quart covered glass casserole dish

2 medium bananas, peeled
½ cup lemon juice
1 pound ground lamb
1 small onion, diced
2 small green pepper, diced
3 cups cooked rice
⅓ cup light cream
2 medium tomatoes, diced
2 teaspoons curry powder
1 teaspoon salt
⅔ cup roasted peanuts

Halve bananas crosswise then lengthwise. Coat well with lemon juice. Set aside. In glass casserole cook ground lamb on **HIGH** for 3½ minutes, stirring once during cooking. Add diced onion and green pepper. Continue cooking on **HIGH** for 3½ minutes or until vegetables are cooked, stirring once during cooking. Drain. To lamb, add rice, cream, tomatoes, curry and salt. Mix well. Top with peanuts and bananas. Cover; cook on **HIGH** for 10 minutes.

My cooking time: ☐

◀ *Spring Ham Casserole*

Tuna Spinach Casserole

TOTAL COOKING TIME: 14 minutes
Serves 4
1½-quart covered glass casserole dish

1 package (10-ounces) frozen chopped spinach
1 can (12½-ounces) solid pack tuna
1 can (10½-ounces) condensed cream of onion soup
1 can (4-ounces) sliced mushrooms, well drained
2 tablespoons lemon juice
½ teaspoon pepper
1 cup grated Cheddar cheese
1 large tomato, sliced for garnish
1 can (3½-ounces) French fried onion rings

In original box, with outer wrapper removed, cook spinach on **HIGH** for 3 minutes, or until spinach separates with a fork. In glass casserole, combine spinach, tuna, soup, mushrooms, lemon juice and pepper. Mix well. Cover; cook on **HIGH** for 8 minutes, or until hot. Top with Cheddar cheese and sliced tomato. Cover; cook on **HIGH** for 3 minutes or until cheese is melted. Sprinkle with onion rings.

My cooking time:

TIP: Excellent entree for luncheon, served with crisp green salad.

Chicken Tetrazzini

TOTAL COOKING TIME: 9 minutes
Serves 4
2-quart covered glass casserole dish

2 cups chopped cooked chicken
4 ounces broken-up spaghetti, cooked
1 package (10-ounces) frozen peas
1 can (10½-ounces) condensed cream of mushroom soup
¼ cup light cream
1 teaspoon garlic powder
¼ cup grated Parmesan cheese
¼ cup bread crumbs

In glass casserole, mix together all ingredients, except cheese and bread crumbs. Cover; cook on **HIGH** for 9 minutes or until hot stirring once during cooking. Sprinkle with Parmesan cheese and bread crumbs.

My cooking time:

Chicken Divan

TOTAL COOKING TIME: 17 minutes
Serves 4
2-quart covered glass casserole dish

2 packages (10-ounces each) frozen broccoli spears in butter sauce
3 cups diced cooked chicken
1 can (10½-ounces) condensed cream of chicken soup
¼ cup sour cream
1 tablespoon lemon juice
1 teaspoon garlic powder
1 teaspoon soy sauce
⅓ cup grated Parmesan cheese
4 tablespoons bread crumbs
4 cups hot cooked rice
Salt to taste

Pierce several holes in broccoli cooking pouches. Cook both pouches together on **HIGH** for 3 minutes, or until stalks separate. Set aside. In large mixing bowl, mix together soup, sour cream, lemon juice, garlic powder and soy sauce, Set aside. Evenly arrange broccoli in dish with spears toward center. Top with half of soup mixture. Lay chicken pieces on top, and spread on remaining soup mixture. Sprinkle with Parmesan cheese and bread crumbs. Cover; cook on **HIGH** for 12 to 14 minutes, or until hot, turning once during cooking.

My cooking time:

Turkey and Peas Casserole

TOTAL COOKING TIME: 15 minutes
Serves 4
1½-quart covered glass casserole dish

1 tablespoon butter
1 tablespoon diced onion
3 cups diced turkey
1 can (10½-ounces) condensed cream of mushroom soup
1 can (10½-ounces) cream of mushroom soup
1 cup grated Cheddar cheese
1 jar (2-ounces) Pimiento strips, diced
2 teaspoons prepared mustard
½ teaspoon garlic powder
Hot cooked rice

In glass casserole, melt butter on **HIGH** for 1 minute, or until melted. Add onion, cook on **HIGH** for 2 minutes or until transparent. Stir in remaining ingredients. Mix well. Cover; cook on **HIGH** for 10 to 12 minutes or until bubbly, stirring once during cooking. Serve over hot rice.

My cooking time:

Zucchini Lasagna

TOTAL COOKING TIME: 18 minutes
Serves 4
1-quart glass casserole dish
2-quart covered glass casserole dish

1 pound lean ground beef
1 can (16-ounces) tomato sauce
1 teaspoon garlic powder
1 teaspoon Italian seasoning
1 teaspoon salt
2 cups ricotta cheese
1 egg, slightly beaten
4 zucchini, thinly sliced lengthwise
½ cup shredded mozzarella cheese

In small glass casserole, cook beef on **HIGH** for 5 minutes of until no longer pink, stirring once during cooking.Drain. Stir tomato sauce, garlic powder, Italian seasoning, and salt into beef. Mix beaten egg with riccota cheese. In large casserole, layer half of zucchini, ricotta cheese and sauce. Repeat layer. Cover; cook on **HIGH** for 10 minutes or until hot, turning once. Sprinkle with cheese. Continue cooking on **HIGH** for 3 minutes, or until cheese melts. Serve hot.

My cooking time:

Ratatouille

TOTAL COOKING TIME: 18 minutes
Serves 4 to 6
3-quart covered glass casserole dish

3 tablespoons olive oil
2 small onions, cut into eighths
2 cloves garlic, finely diced
1 large green pepper, cut into 1-inch cubes
2 medium zucchini, cut into ¼-inch slices
10 Large mushrooms, sliced
1 medium eggplant, cut into 1-inch cubes
4 large tomatoes, quartered
1 teaspoon salt
¼ cup grated Parmesan cheese

In glass casserole, cook olive oil on **HIGH** for 2½ minutes or until hot. Stir in onion, garlic and green pepper. Cover; cook on **HIGH** for 6 minutes or until onion is transparent, stirring twice during cooking. Add zucchini and mushrooms, cover, continue cooking on **HIGH** for 4 minutes. Add eggplant, cover; continue cooking on **HIGH** for 6 minutes. Stir in tomatoes and Parmesan cheese. Cover; continue cooking on **HIGH** for 2 minutes or until tomatoes are hot. Serve hot or cold.

My cooking time:

TIP: A good vegetarian dinner. Serve with toasted garlic bread.

Split Pea Soup

TOTAL COOKING TIME: 4 hours
Makes about 2 quarts
3-quart covered glass casserole dish

- 2 cups dried peas
- ¼ cup celery, thinly sliced
- 1 carrot, thinly sliced
- 1 small onion, diced
- 2 cubes vegetable bouillon
- ¼ pound salt pork, scored
- ¼ teaspoon thyme
- 1½ teaspoons salt
- 1 teaspoon pepper

In glass casserole, soak peas overnight in water. Drain and rinse. Add 6 cups fresh water and remaining ingredients. Cover; cook on **HIGH** for 2 hours then on **MED/DEF** for 2 hours to combine flavors. Remove salt pork before serving.

My cooking time: ☐

Vegetable Soup

TOTAL COOKING TIME: 2 hours
Makes about 2½ quarts
3-quart covered glass casserole dish

- 4 beef shanks
- 6 cups water
- 4 beef bouillon cubes
- 1 can (16-ounces) whole tomatoes
- 1 can (16-ounces) tomato sauce
- 4 carrots, sliced
- 4 stalks celery, sliced
- 2 large onions, cut into bite size chunks
- 2 teaspoons salt
- 1 teaspoon pepper
- 1 teaspoon Italian seasoning (optional)
- 1 can (12-ounces) corn
- 1 package (9-ounces) frozen green beans

In glass casserole, combine all ingredients except corn and green beans. Cover; cook on **HIGH** for 20 minutes, then on **MED/DEF** for 1 hour and 40 minutes. Add green beans and corn during last 40 minutes.

My cooking time: ☐

Old Fashoned Turkey Soup

TOTAL COOKING TIME: 2 hours
Serves 6
3-quart covered glass casserole

- 1 turkey carcass and skin
- Water
- 2 cubes chicken bouillon
- ½ cup pearl barley
- 1 cup chopped onion
- 1 cup chopped celery
- 1 cup diced carrots
- Salt and pepper

Place turkey carcass and skin in glass casserole. Cover with water. Cover; cook on **MED/DEF** for 1 hour. Remove carcass and skin, pick meat from bones and return to broth. Add remaining ingredients and season to taste. Cook on **MED/DEF** for 1 hour longer or until barley is tender.

My cooking time: ☐

Meats

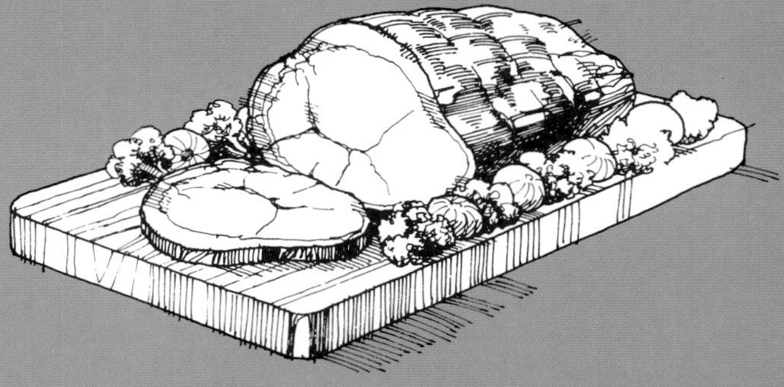

All types of meats are appropriate for microwave cooking. However, just as with conventional cooking, less tender cuts of meat will require longer cooking times at a lower power level than more tender cuts of meat. Below you will find the proper methods for achieving good cooking results for beef, pork, or lamb.

As a General Rule:

- Roast meats uncovered,
- Always use a roasting rack suitable for microwave ovens when roasting to elevate the meat out of the juices that accumulate.
- Roast fat side down and turn once half way through cooking time.
- A meat thermometer, either one contained in the microwave oven or one designed for use in a microwave oven is a must for roasting meats to the perfect degree of doneness.
- Simmer meats covered.
- Plastic cook-in bags may be used when simmering meats.

Microwave Method: Roasting

Use the procedure below in conjunction with the meat roasting chart for roasting all types of meats.

1. Place roast which is completely thawed if previously frozen, fat side down on microwave oven roasting rack or two inverted saucers. Roasting rack should be placed in glass dish to catch juices from meat for gravy. If roast is not elevated out of juices, it may cook unevenly.
2. Cook roast for 5 minutes on power level HIGH.
3. Continue cooking at power level and for time given on Meat Roasting Chart
4. Turn roast fat side up halfway through cooking time.
5. Use a microwave oven meat thermometer whenever possible to assure proper degree of doneness. Cover with foil and allow roast to stand 10 to 20 minutes before carving. This will allow the meat to finish cooking and reach its final doneness. It will also make it easier to carve.

Microwave Method: Ground Meats

Ground meats are tender and can be cooked either in patties or crumbled to add to a casserole. To brown meat for casseroles follow these instructions. A recipe for patties is given in the recipe section.

1. Crumble meat in glass dish or on roasting rack.
2. Cook on power level HIGH for 6 minutes or until it loses its pink color.
3. Drain and add to casserole.

TIP: Brown meat in casserole serving dish. Drain and combine with remaining ingredients in same dish and there are fewer dirty dishes to wash!

MEAT ROASTING CHART

Cut	Weight	Power Level	*Internal Temp.	Approximate Time; per lb.
BEEF				
Rolled Rib Roast	4 lbs.	HIGH	125°F Rare 145°F Med. 160°F Well	7–8 min. 9–10 min. 12–13 min.
Standing Rib Roast	5 lbs.	HIGH	125°F Rare 145°F Med. 160°F Well	6–7 min. 8–9 min. 11–12 min.
Sirloin Tip	4 lbs.	MED/DEF	125°F Rare 145°F Med. 160°F Well	7–8 min. 9–10 min. 12–13 min.
Rump roast Boneless	4 lbs.	MED/DEF	125°F Rare 145°F Med. 160°F Well	10–12 min. 13–15 min. 16–18 min.
Rump roast Bone-in	4 lbs.	MED/DEF	125°F Rare 145°F Med. 160°F Well	9–11 min. 12–14 min. 15–16 min.
PORK				
Rolled, Boneless	4 lbs.	HIGH	160°F Well	12 min.
Loin roast bone-in	4 lbs.	HIGH	155°F Well	11 min.
Ribs	4 lbs.	HIGH		15 min.
HAM				
Boneless-pre-cooked Re-heating only	5 lbs.	HIGH	125°F	10–12 min.
Bone-in, pre-cooked Re-heating only	8 lbs.	HIGH	125°F	9–10 min.
LAMB				
Leg Roast	6 lbs.	MED/DEF	160°F well	11–12 min.
Shoulder, Boneless	4 lbs.	MED/DEF	160°F Well	9–11 min.

* Degree of Doneness is the internal temperature of roast when taken from oven. Another 10F to 15°F increase will occur as meat stands 10 to 20 minutes prior to carving.

Microwave Method: Pot Roasting

If you normally brown the roast before you cook it conventionally, then brown it before you cook it in the microwave.

1. Cut roast into 3 or 4 pieces.
2. Use a covered 2 quart glass dish such as Corning Ware(TM) which is designed for use both on range surfaces and microwave ovens. Dredge roast in flour and brown in oil on conventional surface unit if desired.
3. Add 1 to 1½ cups liquid. Cover and place in microwave oven.
4. Cook on **HIGH** until liquid reaches a simmer approximately 5 minutes.
5. Reduce power level to **MED/DEF** and continue to cook until meat is fork tender. Should take approximately 25 min. per pound. Meat should be turned once or twice during cooking time.
6. If vegetables are added, do so half way through cooking time.
7. Allow to stand 10 minutes before serving.

Microwave Method: Stewing

Just as with a pot roast, if you normally brown the beef cubes when stewing conventionally, then brown them before cooking in the microwave oven.

1. Use a covered 2-quart glass dish such as Corning Ware(TM) which is designed for use on range surfaces and microwave ovens. Dredge meat cubes in seasoned flour and brown in oil on range top if desired.
2. Add 2 cups liquid to meat and cover.
3. Place in microwave oven and cook on **HIGH** until liquid reaches a simmer. Approximately 5 minutes.
4. Reduce power level to **MED/DEF** and continue to cook until meat is fork tender. Should take approximately 1½ to 2 hours. Stir meat several times during cooking time.
5. Vegetables should be added during last half of cooking time.
6. Remove meat and vegetables from liquid and thicken gravy if desired.
7. Return meat and vegetables to gravy and allow to stand 5 minutes before serving.

My Notes:

Microwave Method: Other Meats

COOKING TIMES FOR OTHER MEATS

Meat	Quantity	Power Level	Cooking Time
Hot Dogs	1 2	HIGH HIGH	1 minute 2 minutes
In Buns	1 2	HIGH HIGH	1 min. 15 sec. 2½ minutes
Bacon	3 slices 6 slices	HIGH HIGH	2 minutes 4 minutes
Canadian Bacon	2 slices 4 slices	HIGH HIGH	1 minute 2 minutes
Sausage	2 links 4 links	HIGH HIGH	2 minutes 3 minutes

Cooking Directions:

Hot Dogs: Place on any dish and cook until hot. If cooking in buns, wrap in napkin or paper towel before heating.

Bacon: Place slices on several layers of paper towels and cover with one layer of paper towel. Cook for time recommended on chart or until done as desired.

Canadian Bacon: Place slices on glass dish or plate and heat until hot.

Sausage: Place links on several layers of paper towel and cover with one layer of paper towel. Cook for time recommended on chart.

Chinese Beef with Vegetables

TOTAL COOKING TIME: 11 minutes
Serves 4
2-quart glass casserole dish

1 pound beef flank steak
1 tablespoon teriyaki marinade
1 can (16-ounces) Chinese vegetables, drained
1 can (10¾-ounces) condensed cream of mushroom soup
¼ cup sliced onion
Dash salt and pepper
Hot Oriental noodles

Cut flank steak diagonally across grain into thin slices. Cut slices into 3-inch lengths. Place meat and marinade in glass casserole dish. Cook on **HIGH** for 6 minutes, stirring twice. Combine vegetables, soup, onion, salt and pepper in bowl. Stir into meat to combine. Cover; cook on **HIGH** for 5 minutes, stirring once. Serve over hot noodles.

My cooking time: [ ]

Ground Beef Patties

TOTAL COOKING TIME: 6 minutes
Makes 4
12 x 7-inch glass baking dish
Microwave Roasting Rack

1 pound lean ground beef
1 package (1½-ounces) brown gravy mix

Shape meat into 4 patties about ¾-inch thick. Coat patties on all sides with dry gravy mix. Place patties on rack in baking dish. Cover with wax paper. Cook on **HIGH** for 5 to 6 minutes, turning dish once.

My cooking time: [ ]

Stuffed Cabbage Rolls

TOTAL COOKING TIME: 25 minutes
Serves 4
12 x 7-inch glass baking dish

8 large cabbage leaves
½ cup water
1 pound lean ground beef
1 cup cooked rice
¼ cup chopped onion
1 egg
1 teaspoon salt
¼ teaspoon pepper
1 can (10¾-ounces) condensed tomato soup
1 can (8-ounces) sauerkraut, drained (optional)

In large glass bowl place cabbage leaves and water. Cover with plastic wrap. Cook on **HIGH** for 5 to 7 minutes or until leaves are soft. Combine beef, rice, onion, egg, salt and pepper with 2 tablespoons soup. Divide meat mixture between cabbage leaves; roll and secure with wooden toothpick. Place cabbage rolls, seam side down in baking dish. Combine remaining soup and sauerkraut; pour over cabbage rolls. Cover baking dish loosely with plastic wrap. Cook on **HIGH** for 15 to 20 minutes, turning dish once.

My cooking time: [ ]

◄ *Chinese Beef with Vegetable*

Beef Stew

TOTAL COOKING TIME: 1½ hours
Serves 4 to 6
2-quart covered glass casserole dish

1½ to 2 pounds lean beef stew meat
1 envelope (1½-ounces) beef stew seasoning mix
1 can (8-ounces) tomato sauce
2 cups water
3 potatoes, peeled and cubed
2 carrots, peeled and sliced
1 onion, quartered

In glass casserole combine meat, seasoning, tomato sauce, and water. Cover; cook on **HIGH** for 10 minutes, or until liquid comes to a boil. Reduce power; cook on **MED/DEF** for 45 minutes. Add vegetables and continue to cook on **MED/DEF** for 30 to 45 minutes, until meat is tender.

My cooking time:

Pot Roast

TOTAL COOKING TIME: 2 hours
Serves 4 to 6
3-quart covered glass casserole dish

3 to 4 pounds beef chuck pot roast
1 envelope (1½-ounces) onion soup mix
1 can (10¾-ounces) condensed beef broth
1 onion, thinly sliced
6 small potatoes, peeled
4 carrots, peeled and sliced
2 stalks celery, cut diagonally
½ pound fresh mushrooms

Place roast in glass casserole dish. Sprinkle mix over roast; add onions. Pour in soup; cover. Cook on **HIGH** for 10 minutes or until liquid begins to boil. Reduce power, cook on **MED/DEF** for 1½ to 2 hours, or until meat is fork tender. Add remaining vegetables during last 30 minutes of cooking.

My cooking time:

Short Ribs

TOTAL COOKING TIME: 1 hour 45 minutes
Serves 4
3-quart covered glass casserole dish

3 to 4 pounds short ribs
Oil
1 can (10¾-ounces) condensed golden mushroom soup
¾ cup red wine
2 stalks celery, cut into 4-inch pieces
1 jar (4½-ounces) whole mushrooms with liquid
¼ cup flour
Water

Conventionally brown short ribs in oil on surface unit. Place in glass casserole. Combine soup, wine and celery and pour over ribs. Cover; cook on **MED/DEF** for 1 hour and 45 minutes. Remove meat and celery from sauce and discard celery. Mix flour with enough water to make a paste and stir into sauce. Add mushrooms, cook on **HIGH** for 5 minutes or until thick. Pour sauce over ribs.

My cooking time:

Corned Beef and Cabbage

TOTAL COOKING TIME: 1 hour 40 minutes
Serves 6 to 8
3-quart covered glass casserole dish

3 pounds corned beef
Water to cover
1 large cabbage, cut into 8 wedges

Place corned beef in glass casserole, add water to cover. Cover; cook on **MED/DEF** for 1½ hours or until corned beef is tender. Remove meat to serving platter. Add cabbage to corned beef broth and cook on **HIGH** for 10 minutes. Slice corned beef and serve with cabbage.

My cooking time:

◄*Pot Roast*

Beef and Peppers

TOTAL COOKING TIME: 16 minutes
Serves 4
12 x 7-inch glass baking dish

1½ pounds rib eye steaks
⅓ cup steak sauce
2 cans (4-ounces each) sliced mushrooms, drained
1 green pepper, cut in strips
1 onion, thinly sliced
1 tablespoon chopped parsley

Brush steaks with steak sauce and place in baking dish. Cover with wax paper. Cook on **HIGH** for 8 minutes. Add mushrooms, pepper, and onion; recover. Cook on HIGH for 6 to 8 minutes. Sprinkle with parsley to serve.

My cooking time: ☐

Swedish Meatballs

TOTAL COOKING TIME: 17 minutes
Serves 4
3-quart covered glass casserole dish
4 cup glass measuring cup

1¼ pounds ground beef
2 eggs, slightly beaten
¾ cup milk
½ cup bread crumbs
½ cup finely chopped onion
¼ cup margarine or butter, melted
½ teaspoon salt
⅛ teaspoon each nutmeg, allspice and cardamom
1 can (10¾ ounces) condensed cream of mushroom soup
1 can (10½-ounces) condensed beef bouillon
1 cup sour cream

In large mixing bowl, combine eggs, milk and bread crumbs. Stir in ground beef, salt, nutmeg, allspice and cardamom. The mixture will be soft. Shape into 1-inch balls and place in glass casserole. Cover; cook on **HIGH** for 10 minutes or until no longer pink, gently stir twice during cooking. In glass measuring cup, combine onion and butter. Cook on **HIGH** for 1½ minutes or until onion is soft. Stir in mushroom soup and bouillon; pour over cooked meat balls. Cook on **HIGH** for 5 to 7 minutes or until sauce is hot. Stir in sour cream and serve.

My cooking time: ☐

Old Fashioned Beef Stroganoff

TOTAL COOKING TIME: 1 hour 20 minutes
Serves 6
3-quart covered glass casserole dish

2 pounds beef round steak
1½ cups water
1 jar (4½-ounces) whole mushrooms
2 cubes beef bouillon
1 teaspoon salt
¼ cup flour
1 cup sour cream

Slice beef into very thin slices about 2 inches long. Place beef in casserole and add water, mushrooms with juice, bouillon cubes and salt. Cover; cook on **MED/DEF** for 1 hour and 15 minutes. Combine flour with enough water to make a paste. Stir into beef mixture and cook on **HIGH** for 5 minutes. Stir in sour cream and serve.

My cooking time: ☐

Mexican Shredded Beef

TOTAL COOKING TIME: 2 hours
Serves 6 to 8
3-quart covered glass casserole dish

2 pounds beef brisket
1 can (8-ounces) tomato sauce
1 package (1¼-ounces) taco seasoning mix

Place brisket in glass casserole dish and add enough water to cover. Cover; cook on **MED/DEF** for 2 hours. Turn half way through cooking. Reserve ½ cup cooking liquid. Cut brisket in half across grain. Pull meat apart with forks to shred. Stir in ½ cup liquid, tomato sauce and taco seasoning. Cover; cook on **HIGH** for 5 minutes, or until hot. Use for tacos, burritos or enchiladas.

My cooking time: ☐

◀ *Beef and Peppers*

Stirred Steak and Vegetables

TOTAL COOKING TIME: 11 minutes
Serves 4
2½-quart covered glass casserole dish

1¼ pounds beef sirloin steak, cut in bite size pieces
1 small onion, thinly sliced
1 green pepper, thinly sliced
½ pound fresh mushrooms, sliced
1 can (8-ounces) tomato sauce
¼ cup soy sauce
1 tablespoon vinegar
1 clove garlic, crushed
½ teaspoon powdered ginger

Place meat in glass casserole. Cook on **HIGH** for 4 to 5 minutes until no longer pink, stir occasionally. Top beef with sliced vegetables. Combine tomato sauce, soy sauce, vinegar, garlic, and ginger to make sauce; pour over vegetables. Cover; cook on **HIGH** for 5 to 6 minutes until vegetabes are crisp-tender. Allow to stand for 5 minutes before serving. Arrange vegetables in center of platter, ring with meat and top with sauce.

My cooking time: ☐

Hot Chili Con Carne

TOTAL COOKING TIME: 45 minutes
Serves 4
3-quart covered glass casserole dish

- 1 pound lean ground beef
- 1 can (30-ounces) chili beans
- 1 can (16-ounces) whole tomatoes
- 1 can (7-ounces) chopped green chiles
- 1 large onion, diced
- 2 tablespoons chili powder
- 1¼ teaspoons salt
- ½ teaspoon garlic powder
- ¼ teaspoon oregano
- ¼ teaspoon cumin
- ¼ teaspoon black pepper

In glass casserole, cook ground beef on **HIGH** for 5 minutes, or until no longer pink. Drain. Add remaining ingredients. Cover; cook on **MED/DEF** for 40 minutes, or until flavors are combined.

My cooking time: ☐

Sweet 'n Sour Stuffed Cabbage

TOTAL COOKING TIME: 15 to 20 minutes
Serves 6–8
3-quart covered glass casserole dish

- 1 large head cabbage, cored
- 1 pound lean ground beef
- 1 cup minute rice
- 1 cup raisins; divided
- 1 onion diced; divided
- 2 teaspoons salt; divided
- 2 cans (16-ounces each) tomato sauce
- 3 tablespoon lemon juice
- 2 tablespoons brown sugar
- 1 cup gingersnap crumbs
- 2 teaspoons salt
- Water

Wrap whole cabbage in plastic wrap and cook on **HIGH** for 10 minutes or until tender, but still slightly firm. Meanwhile, combine beef, rice, ½ cup raisins, ½ cup onions and 1 teaspoon salt. Using the larger outer cabbage leaves place about 2 tablespoons of mixture on each cabbage leaf, roll securely and place in glass casserole, seam side down. Chop remaining cabbage and place on top of stuffed cabbage. For sauce, combine remaining raisins, onion and salt with tomato sauce, lemon juice, brown sugar and gingersnap crumbs. Pour over stuffed cabbage and add water to cover (about 1 cup). Cover; cook on **HIGH** for 15 to 20 minutes, turning dish once.

My cooking time: ☐

Special Pot Roast

TOTAL COOKING TIME: 2 hours
Serves 4
3-quart covered glass casserole dish

- 3 to 4 pounds beef chuck pot roast
- 1 envelope (1½-ounces) onion soup mix
- 1 can (10½-ounces) condensed beef broth
- 1 onion, thinly sliced
- ½ pound yellow squash, sliced
- ½ pound zucchini, sliced
- Salt and pepper to taste

Place roast in glass casserole dish. Sprinkle soup mix over roast. Add onions. Pour in beef broth. Cover; cook on **MED/DEF** for 2 hours or until meat is tender. Add remaining vegetables during last 45 minutes of cooking.

My cooking time: ☐

Hungrian Goulash

TOTAL COOKING TIME: 1¼ hours
Serves 4
3-quart covered glass casserole dish

- 2 pounds beef stew meat
- Flour
- Oil
- 2 cans (16-ounces each) tomato sauce
- 2 onions, thinly sliced
- 2 tablespoons paprika
- 1 tablespoon pepper
- 1 tablespoon salt
- Hot cooked egg noodles
- Sour cream

Dredge meat in flour. Conventionally brown meat in oil on surface unit. Place browned meat in glass casserole. Add remaining ingredients. Cover, cook on **MED/DEF** for 1¼ hours or until meat is tender. Serve over hot noodles, garnish with sour cream.

My cooking time: ☐

◄ *Stirred Steak and Vegetables*

Meatball Stew

TOTAL COOKING TIME: 32 minutes
Serves 6
9-inch glass pie plate
3-quart glass casserole dish

1 pound lean ground beef.
1 egg
½ cup fine bread crumbs
2 tablespoons onion soup mix
1 can (16-ounces) sliced carrots, drained
1 can (16-ounces) whole white potatoes, drained
1 can (8-ounces) small white onions, drained
1 package (10-ounces) frozen peas
1 can (10¾-ounces) condensed tomato soup
1 can (10¾-ounces) condensed beef broth

Combine meat, egg, bread crumbs, and soup mix Shape into 12 balls and arrange in a circle in 9-inch glass pie plate. Cover with wax paper. Cook on **HIGH** for 9 to 12 minutes, turning dish once. Combine vegetables and soups in casserole; add meatballs. Cover; cook on **MED/DEF** for 15 to 20 minutes, stirring once.

My cooking time: ☐

Beef Bourguignon

TOTAL COOKING TIME: 1 hour 20 minutes
Serves 4–6
3-quart covered glass casserole dish

2 pounds beef stew meat
½ cup flour
Oil
1 cup beef bouillon
2 cups burgundy, divided
1 pound pearl onions, peeled
4 carrots, cut jullienne style
1 tablespoon chopped parsley
2 cloves garlic, pressed or chopped
1½ teaspoons salt
1 package (10-ounces) frozen peas
1 jar (4½-ounces) whole mushrooms
½ cup flour

Dredge stew meat in flour and brown coventionally on surface unit. Place browned meat in glass casserole. Add bouillon, 1½ cups burgundy, onions, carrots, parsley, garlic, salt and water to cover. Cover; cook on **HIGH** for 1¼ hours, or until meat is tender. Add peas and mushrooms during last half hour of cooking. Remove from broth. For sauce, combine ¼ cup flour with enough water to make a paste. Add to meat stock and stir well. Cook on **HIGH** for 5 minutes, or until boiling. Stir in ½ cup burgundy; pour over meat and vegetables.

My cooking time: ☐

Old Fashioned Beef Stew

TOTAL COOKING TIME: 2 hours
Serves 4
3-quart covered glass casserole dish

2 pounds lean beef stew meat
2 beef bouillon cubes
2 cups water
4 small potatoes, peeled and sliced
2 carrots, peeled and sliced
8 boiling onions
Salt and pepper to taste

In glass casserole, combine meat, seasoning mix, bouillon cubes, and water. Cover; cook on **HIGH** for 10 minutes or until liquid boils. Reduce power, cook on **MED/DEF** for 1½–2 hours or until meat is fork tender. Add remaining ingredients during last hour of cooking. Season with salt and pepper to taste.

My cooking time: ☐

◄ *Meatball Stew*

Meat Loaf

TOTAL COOKING TIME: 15 minutes
Serves 4 to 6
9 x 5-inch glass loaf dish

¾ pound ground beef
¼ pound ground pork
1 egg
1 can (8-ounces) tomato sauce
¾ cups fresh bread crumbs
1 teaspoon Worcestershire sauce
½ teaspoon savory (optional)

TOPPING
¼ cup catsup
2 tablespoons Worcestershire sauce

Combine all ingredients except topping; shape into loaf dish. Combine topping ingredients; spread over loaf. Cover with wax paper. Cook on **HIGH** for 15 minutes, turning dish once. Allow to stand 10 minutes before serving.

My cooking time:

Swiss Steak

TOTAL COOKING TIME: 1¼ hours
Serves 4
3-quart covered glass casserole dish

2 pounds beef round steak, cut into serving pieces
Flour
Oil
1 onion, sliced
1 can (15-ounces) tomato sauce
1 teaspoon salt
½ teaspoon pepper

Cut beef into serving pieces. Dredge in flour and brown conventionally in oil. Place in glass casserole. Brown onion conventionally in oil and place on top of meat. Add tomato sauce, salt and pepper. Cover; cook on **MED/DEF** for 1¼ hours or until meat is tender.

My cooking time:

Onion Steak

TOTAL COOKING TIME: 1 hour
Serves 4 to 6
14 x 20-inch cook-in-bag
12 x 8-inch glass casserole dish

1½ pounds boneless beef round steak, cut into serving pieces
Meat tenderizer
1 can (10¾-ounces) condensed cream of mushroom soup
1 medium onion, sliced
2 tablespoons dry onion soup mix
1 tablespoon Worcestershire sauce
Chopped parsley

Score both sides of steak pieces diagonally, about 1-inch apart. Sprinkle both sides of meat with meat tenderizer. Place steak in bag. Combine remaining ingredients in bowl. Pour into bag, turning bag several times to mix. Close bag with rubber band, string, or ¾-inch strip cut from open end of bag. Make six half-inch slits in top. Cook on **HIGH** for 5 minutes. Reduce power, cook on **MED/DEF** for 50 to 60 minutes, turning dish once. Sprinkle with parsley to serve.

My cooking time:

TIP: This recipe also works well in tightly covered casserole dish.

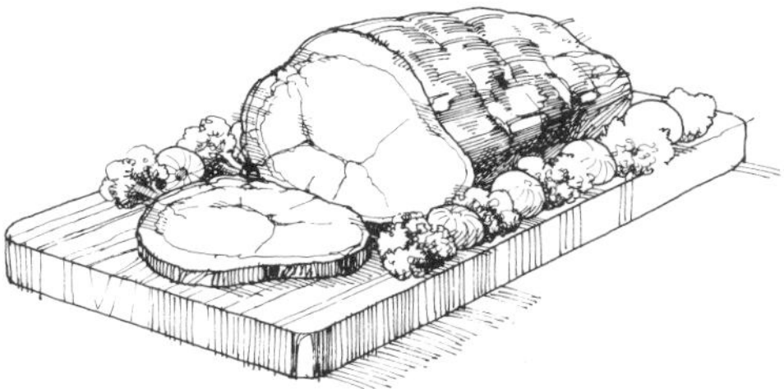

◄*Meat Loaf*

Brisket in Horseradish Sauce

TOTAL COOKING TIME: 1 hour 40 minutes
Serves 4 to 6
3-quart covered glass casserole dish

3 pounds brisket
Oil
1 onion, sliced
1 bay leaf
2 beef bouillon cubes
Water
Horseradish Sauce

Conventionally sear brisket in oil on both sides on surface unit. Place seared brisket in glass casserole and add onion, bay leaf, bouillon and enough water to cover. Cover; cook on **MED/DEF** for 1½ hours, or until meat is tender. Slice diagonally and serve with Horseradish Sauce.

HORSERADISH SAUCE
2 cups strained meat stock
1 medium onion, diced
¾ cup prepared white horseradish
¼ cup sugar
¼ cup butter
3 tablespoons flour
¼ cup apple cider vinegar
2 whole cloves

In glass measuring cup, combine all ingredients and cook on **HIGH** for 10 minutes, or until thickened. Stir once during cooking. Remove cloves before serving.

My cooking time: ☐

Hearty Braised Beef

TOTAL COOKING TIME: 1 hour 33 minutes
Serves 4
3-quart covered glass casserole dish

6 slices bacon
2 pounds beef round steak, cut into serving pieces
2 onions, sliced
2 beef bouillon cubes
1½ cups water
¼ cup flour

Place bacon slices between layers of paper towels and cook on **HIGH** for 6 minutes or until crisp. Meanwhile, pound beef with mallet or edge of saucer, then place in glass casserole. Crumble bacon and add to meat along with onion, bouillon and water. Cover; cook on **MED/DEF** for 1 hour 30 minutes or until meat is tender. Remove meat from stock to serving platter. Combine flour with enough water to make a paste. Stir into stock and cook on **HIGH** for 3 minutes or until thickened; pour over meat.

My cooking time: ☐

Dinner in a Pot

TOTAL COOKING TIME: 40 minutes
Serves 4
3-quart covered glass casserole dish

4 thick pork chops
Flour
Oil
4 large potatoes, sliced
2 cups milk
1 onion, sliced
1 cube chicken bouillon
Salt and pepper

Dredge pork chops in flour and brown conventionally in oil on surface unit. Place browned pork chops in glass casserole. Add remaining ingredients. Cover; cook on **MED/DEF** for 40 minutes, or until chops are tender.

My cooking time: ☐

Country Style Spareribs

TOTAL COOKING TIME: 1 hour 45 minutes
Serves 4
3-quart covered glass casserole dish

3 pounds "country style" pork loin spareribs
2 cups hot tap water
SAUCE
1 can (8-ounces) tomato sauce
½ cup chopped onion
3 tablespoons brown sugar
2 tablespoons lemon juice
1 teaspoon prepared mustard
½ teaspoon liquid smoke

Place meat in casserole, bone side up. Add water. Cover; cook on **MED/DEF** for 90 minutes, turning dish after 45 minutes. Combine sauce ingredients. Drain liquid from ribs. Pour sauce over top of ribs. Cook on **MED/DEF** for 10 to 15 minutes until sauce has dried on top.

My cooking time: ☐

Padilla's Chili Verde

TOTAL COOKING TIME: 40 minutes
Serves 4
3-quart covered glass casserole dish

2 pounds pork shoulder, cut into 1 inch cubes
Flour
Oil
1 small onion, diced
6 garlic cloves, chopped or pressed
1 can (7-ounces) diced green chiles
1 can (8-ounces) tomato sauce
1 cup water
2 teaspoons salt
½ teaspoon pepper

Dredge pork cubes in flour. Conventionally brown in oil on surface unit. Place browned pork cubes in glass casserole dish. Combine remaining ingredients and pour over pork. Stir well. Cover; cook on **MED/DEF** for 40 minutes, or until meat is tender.

My cooking time: ☐

Saucy Braised Pork Chops

TOTAL COOKING TIME: 40 minutes
Serves 4
3-quart covered glass casserole dish

8 thin pork chops
Flour
Oil
1 can (10½-ounces) condensed cream of chicken soup
1 small onion, chopped
¼ cup dry white wine

Dredge chops in flour and brown coventionally on surface unit. Place browned chops in glass casserole. Combine soup, onion and wine and pour over chops. Cover; cook on **MED/DEF** for 40 minutes or until chops are tender.

My cooking time: ☐

NOTE: This recipe is also excellent substituting cream of asparagus soup for cream of chicken soup.

Pork Roast and Sauerkraut

TOTAL COOKING TIME: 40 minutes
Serves 4
3-quart covered glass casserole dish

2½ to 3 pounds pork shoulder roast, boned and tied
1 jar (32-ounces) sauerkraut, drained and rinsed well
1 large onion, thinly sliced
½ teaspoon pepper
2 cups chicken broth
2 teaspoons caraway seeds
1 bay leaf
1 teaspoon salt

In glass casserole, combine all ingredients except pork roast. Mix well, then place pork roast on top. Cover; cook on **HIGH** for 40 minutes or until tender.

My cooking time: ☐

TIP: If desired, conventionally brown roast in oil on surface unit before cooking.

Hearty German Casserole

TOTAL COOKING TIME: 20 minutes
Serves 4
2-quart covered glass casserole dish

3 cups coarsely chopped cabbage
2 medium apples, chopped
1 can (10¾-ounces) condensed cream of onion soup
⅓ cup packed brown sugar
2 teaspoons carraway seeds
4 smoked pork chops
1 pound precooked Polish sausage

In large glass casserole combine cabbage, apples, soup, sugar, and caraway seeds. Arrange chops and sausage over top. Cover tightly. Cook on **MED/DEF** for 15 to 20 minutes until cabbage is tender.

My cooking time:

Ham Loaf

TOTAL COOKING TIME: 20 minutes
Serves 4
9 x 5-inch glass loaf dish

1½ pounds ground cooked ham
2 eggs
½ cup soft bread crumbs
¼ cup chopped onion
¼ cup chopped green pepper
¼ cup milk
⅓ cup packed brown sugar
1 tablespoon prepared mustard
⅓ cup pineapple juice

Combine ham, eggs, bread crumbs, onion, pepper, and milk; mix thoroughly. Shape into loaf dish. Combine brown sugar and mustard; spread over loaf. Pour pineapple juice over all. Cook on **HIGH** for 5 minutes. Reduce power, cook on **MED/DEF** for 10 to 15 minutes until firm.

My cooking time:

Ham and Yam Dinner

TOTAL COOKING TIME: 15 minutes
Serves 4 to 6
12 x 7-inch glass baking dish

1 slice fully-cooked ham, 1 to 2-inches thick
1 can (16-ounces) sliced yams, drained
1 can (8-ounces) crushed pineapple
½ cup orange marmalade

Score edges of ham slice to prevent curling. Place ham in glass baking dish. Arrange yams over ham. Spoon on crushed pineapple and marmalade. Cover dish loosely with plastic wrap. Cook on **HIGH** for 12 to 15 minutes until heated through. Let stand 5 minutes before serving.

My cooking time:

Stuffed Pork Chops

TOTAL COOKING TIME: 49 minutes
Serves 4
12 x 7-inch glass baking dish

4 pork chops, 1-inch thick, cut with pocket
1 package (6-ounces) pork flavored stuffing mix
1½ cups apple juice
½ cup raisins
Salt and pepper
1 can (10¾-ounces) condensed cream of mushroom soup

To make pocket in chop, cut a slit from outer edge to bone. In large measuring cup combine apple juice, raisins, and vegetable-seasoning packet from stuffing mix. Cook on **HIGH** for 3 to 4 minutes to bring to a boil. Reduce power, continue to cook on **MED/DEF** for 5 minutes. Stir in crumb mix to moisten. Loosely stuff each pocket with stuffing; secure with wooden toothpick. Arrange chops in glass baking dish with meatiest portions toward the outer edge. Season to taste with salt and pepper. Spoon soup over chops. Cover loosely with plastic wrap. Cook on **MED/DEF** for 30 to 40 minutes turning dish once.

My cooking time:

◄ *Hearty German Casserole*

Glazed Fruited Pork Chops

TOTAL COOKING TIME: 29 minutes
Serves 4
9-inch glass baking dish
2-cup glass measuring cup

4 pork chops, center cut pork loin (about 1½ to 2-pounds)
4 slices apple
4 slices orange
Dash cinnamon
Dash ground cloves
1 can (10½-ounces) condensed beef broth
1 tablespoon orange juice concentrate
1 tablespoon cornstarch

In glass baking dish arrange pork chops with meatiest portions toward outside of dish. Place apple and orange slice on each chop; sprinkle with cinnamon and cloves. Add soup and sugar. Cover; cook on **MED/DEF** for 15 to 20 minutes, turning dish once. Lift chops from dish, and arrange on platter. Combine orange juice concentrate and cornstarch in 2-cup glass measuring cup. Strain juices remaining in baking dish into measuring cup to measure 1½ cups, stirring to blend. Cook on **HIGH** for 3 to 4 minutes until slightly thickened. Pour glaze over chops.

My cooking time: ☐

Sunday Brunch Bacon

TOTAL COOKING TIME: 15 minutes
Serves 6 to 8
10 x 6-inch plastic cook-in-bag
9-inch glass baking dish

2 to 3 pound whole Canadian bacon
Whole cloves
2 cans (8¼-ounces each) sliced pineapple, reserve syrup
2 tablespoons brown sugar
1 teaspoon prepared mustard
¼ teaspoon powdered ginger
Maraschino cherries

Score surface of bacon with diagonal slashes. Stud bacon with whole cloves. Place bacon in plastic cook-in-bag. Combine pineapple syrup, sugar, mustard, and ginger; pour into bag. Allow bacon to marinate at least one hour at room temperature or over night in refrigerator. Place bag in baking dish; loosely fold over top of bag. Cook on **HIGH** for 10 to 15 minutes or until warmed through. Arrange bacon on serving platter surrounded by pineapple slices and cherries. Pour hot sauce over bacon, pineapple, and cherries.

My cooking time: ☐

TIP: Allow bacon to marinate over night for a succulent treat on Sunday morning.

Chicken Livers and Wine Sauce

TOTAL COOKING TIME: 33 minutes
Serves 4
2-quart glass casserole

6 slices bacon, cut in 1-inch pieces
½ cup chopped onion
1 pound chicken livers
1 pound fresh mushrooms, sliced
1 green pepper, sliced
1 can (8-ounces) tomato sauce
½ cup Chianti wine
2 tablespoons soy sauce
Salt and pepper to taste
3 cups hot cooked rice

Place onion and bacon in glass casserole. Cover with paper towel. Cook on **HIGH** for 10 to 12 minutes until bacon is brown. Add livers; cook on **HIGH** for 5 to 6 minutes until liver is light in color. Add mushrooms and pepper to casserole. Add tomato sauce, wine and soy sauce; season to taste. Cook on **MED/DEF** for 10 to 15 minutes, stirring occasionally. Spoon over hot cooked rice.

My cooking time: ☐

◀*Sunday Brunch Bacon*

Sweet and Sour Pork

TOTAL COOKING TIME: 40 minutes
Serves 4
3-quart covered glass casserole dish

3 pounds pork shoulder, cut into cubes
Flour
2 teaspoons ground ginger
Oil
¼ cup flour
1 can (8-ounces) pineapple chunks
¼ cup vinegar
¼ cup soy sauce
1½ teaspoon Worchestershire sauce
⅓ cup sugar
1½ teaspoons salt
½ teaspoon pepper
1 green pepper, sliced
1 can (8-ounces) water chestnuts, sliced
2 tablespoons chili sauce

Dredge pork in mixture of flour and ginger. Conventionally brown in oil on surface unit. Combine ¼ cup flour with pineapple juice and add water to measure 1 cup. Add vinegar, soy, sauce, Worcestershire sauce, sugar, salt and pepper. Cook on **HIGH** for 7 minutes or until thickened. Add meat. Cover; cook on **MED/DEF** for 40 minutes or until meat is tender. Add green pepper, water chestnuts and chili sauce. Cook covered on **HIGH** for 10 minutes. Serve over fluffy rice.

My cooking time: ☐

Marinated Lamb Roast

TOTAL COOKING TIME: 45 to 60 minutes
12 x 7-inch glass baking dish
Microwave roasting rack

6 to 7 pound leg of lamb, boned, rolled, and tied
MARINADE
½ cup olive oil
¼ cup dry white wine
¼ cup lemon juice
2 cloves garlic, crushed
1 teaspoon salt
½ teaspoon pepper
¼ teaspoon *each* rosemary, thyme, oregano

MINT SAUCE
1 cup white wine vinegar
¼ cup sugar
¼ cup chopped fresh mint leaves
Dash of salt

Combine marinade ingredients in heavy plastic bag. Place lamb in bag. Allow to marinate at least 4 hours, or overnight, if possible. Place roast on microwave roasting rack fat side down. Cook on **MED/DEF** for 45 to 60 minutes, turning fat side up after half of the cooking time. Allow to stand, tented with foil, 10 to 15 minutes before serving. Serve with mint sauce.
For mint sauce combine ingredients in 2-cup glass measuring cup. Cook on **MED/DEF** for 5 to 6 minutes until boiling. Cool to room temperature to serve with roast.

My cooking time: ☐

Shish Kabob

TOTAL COOKING TIME: 11 to 13 minutes
Serves 4
12 x 7-inch glass baking dish
Microwave roasting rack

½ cup mint jelly
¼ cup oil
¼ cup wine vinegar
2 pound lamb shoulder cut into 1-inch cubes
8 small onions or shallots
8 large fresh mushrooms
8 cherry tomatoes
8 wooden skewers

In covered glass dish, cook jelly, oil and vinegar on **HIGH** for 1 minute or until jelly is dissolved. Add meat, and marinate for at least 4 hours; or over night if possible. Alternate lamb cubes and vegetables on skewers. Place on roasting rack in glass baking dish. Cover; cook on **HIGH** for 10 minutes or until lamb is desired degree of doneness.

My cooking time: ☐

Poultry

Poultry cooked in the microwave oven is juicy, tender and a definite time saver. Diced chicken for a salad or a sandwich is ready in minutes and can be cooked in the time it takes to assemble the rest of the ingredients.

As a General Rule:

- All poultry adapts well to the microwave oven.
- Cook whole birds uncovered on a roasting rack.
- Cook on power level HIGH
- Arrange poultry parts properly in dish for best cooking results.
- Poultry plus a sauce is an excellent combination and adds flavor along with color.
- If your conventional recipe calls for browning the chicken pieces before cooking, brown them before cooking in the microwave oven.

Microwave Method:

All poultry is a tender type of meat and adapts well to microwave cooking. Chickens may require a glaze or coating mixture to give extra color because they cook so quickly that natural browning doesn't take place. To prepare the different types of poultry follow our suggestions given below.

To Cook Poultry Pieces:

1. Place chicken skin side down in shallow glass dish as recommended in the illustration below.

Roun Dish
Chicken parts

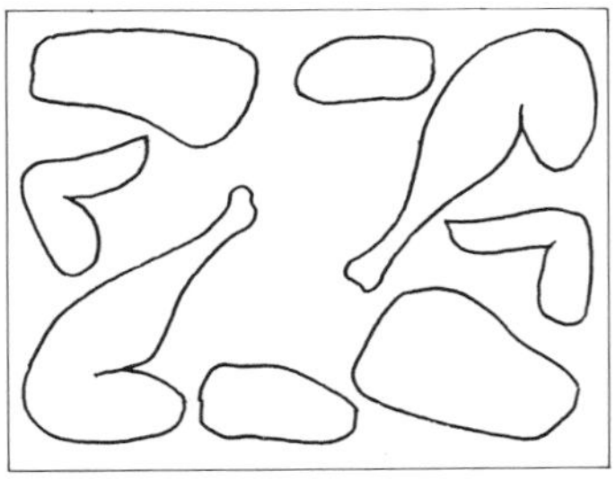

Square Dish
Chicken parts

2. Cook, covered with wax paper on power level HIGH for approximately 8—10 minutes per pound or until thoroughly cooked. Turn chicken over halfway through cooking time. Remove from oven and allow to stand 5 to 10 minutes before serving.

When to Add Sauce:

- Savory sauces should be added at beginning of cooking time.
- Sweet sauce should be added before turning pieces over.

TIP: Microwave cooking does not evaporate the liquid from sauces as in conventional cooking. Therefore increase the amount of cornstarch to thicken a sweet sauce, or decrease the amount of water in a savory sauce.

Cooking Whole Birds

General Instructions:

Turkey, chicken, duckling, goose, and Rock Cornish game hens can be roasted in microwave ovens using common techniques:
From fully defrosted state, rinse and pat dry. Stuff bird, if desired. Close neck opening with wooden skewers; tie legs and wings loosely with string. Place bird, breast side down, on microwave roasting rack, trivet, or inverted saucers in appropriate sized baking dish. Cook, uncovered, for half of the estimated cooking time (see chart). Drain off excess drippings if needed. Turn bird breast side up, baste with drippings, butter, or seasoned glaze. Continue to cook, uncovered, for remaining time. On larger birds watch carefully for brown spots which indicate over cooking. If they occur, cover spots with small pieces of foil, secured with wooden pick to prevent over cooking. Food probe or *microwave thermometer* inserted in thickest part of thigh should read about 170° at the end of cooking time. Remove from oven. Cover bird with foil tent and allow to stand 10 to 15 minutes or until the thermometer reads 180°-185°F. Smaller birds are done when the legs move freely.

POULTRY ROASTING CHART

Type	Weight	Power Level	Approx. Time per Pound
CHICKEN			
Whole, Fryer	2–3 lbs.	HIGH	9 min.
Whole, Roaster	4–5 lbs.	HIGH	9 min.
Parts	1 lb. (3 to 4 pieces)	HIGH	8 min.
Whole Turkey	10–12 lbs.	HIGH	8 min.
Cornish Game Hen	1–2 lbs.	HIGH	9 min.
Duckling	4–5 lbs.	HIGH	9 min.
Goose	9–11 lbs.	HIGH	6 min.

NOTE: Total cooking time is about the same for stuffed or unstuffed poultry. Times are approximate and may vary due to the starting temperature.

1973
POMAGNE

Festive Game Hens

TOTAL COOKING TIME: 20 to 25 minutes
Serves 2
12 x 7½-inch glass baking dish
Microwave roasting rack

2 Rock Cornish game hens
GLAZE
½ cup apricot jam
1 tablespoon soy sauce
1 teaspoon dry mustard
1 teaspoon orange peel
Sour cream for garnish, if desired

Prepare birds for cooking as indicated in general instructions. Arrange in dish, brush hens with glaze; cover with wax paper. Base cooking time on combined weight of hens being cooked. Cook on **HIGH** for 9 minutes per pound. After half of the cooking period, turn hens over; baste with glaze, cover and continue to cook. When done, the legs should move freely and juices run clear. Allow to stand, covered, 10 minutes before serving.

My cooking time: ☐

TIP: Skin may be further browned under broiler.

Roast Turkey

TOTAL COOKING TIME: about 2 hours
Serves 10 to 12
13 x 9-inch baking dish
Microwave roasting rack

10 to 12 pound turkey (no larger, for best results)
GLAZE
¼ cup honey
1 teaspoon Worcestershire sauce
1 teaspoon soy sauce

Carefully follow general instructions for preparing and cooking whole bird. Cook on **HIGH** for 8 minutes per pound. Determine doneness by following general instructions. Be sure to allow 10 to 12 minutes tented with foil standing time for turkey to finish cooking.

My cooking time: ☐

TIP: Use paper towels as hot pads to turn turkey.

Duckling A'la Orange

TOTAL COOKING TIME: about 1 hour
Serves 3 to 4
11 x 7-inch glass baking dish
Microwave roasting rack

4 to 5 pound duckling
1 whole orange, quartered
1 onion, quartered
2 stalk celery
½ cup orange marmalade

Prepare duckling for cooking following general instructions. Fill cavity with orange, onion and celery. Truss. Before cooking, generously pierce skin with tines of a fork to allow fat to drain into dish during cooking. While cooking, drain excess fat from dish to prevent spatters and smoking. Cook on **HIGH** for 9 minutes per pound. Glaze with marmalade after half the cooking period.

My cooking time: ☐

TIP: Skin may be further browned and crisped under broiler, if desired.

◀ *Festive Game Hens*

affiné au marc de bourgogne
NET WT 9 OZ PRODUCT OF FRANCE

Onion and Cheese Chicken Bake

TOTAL COOKING TIME: 12 to 13 minutes
Serve 6
12 x 7½-inch glass baking dish

6 chicken breasts, skinned and boned (about 2 pounds after boning)
4 tablespoons butter
1 teaspoon *each* seasoned salt and pepper
½ pound fresh mushrooms, sliced
1 can (3-ounces) French-fried onion rings
½ cup grated Jack or Swiss cheese

Melt butter in baking dish on **MED/DEF** for 1 minute or until melted, add seasonings. Roll chicken in seasoned butter to coat and arrange in dish. Cover with wax paper; cook on **HIGH** for 5 to 6 minutes. Turn pieces over, top with mushrooms. Continue to cook on **HIGH** for 4 minutes. Sprinkle with onion rings and grated cheese. Cook on **HIGH** for 2 to 3 minutes or until cheese bubbles.

My cooking time: ☐

Roast Goose

TOTAL COOKING TIME: about 1½ hours
Serves 8 to 10
13 x 9-inch glass baking dish
Microwave roasting rack

9 to 10 pound domestic goose
8 dried apricots
8 dried prunes
1 apple, quartered
1 teaspoon salt
1 cup plum preserves, if desired

Prepare goose for cooking following general instructions. Fill cavity with apricots, prunes, apple, and salt. Truss. Before cooking, generously pierce skin with tines of fork to allow fat to drain into dish during cooking. While cooking, drain excess fat from dish to prevent spatter. Cook on **HIGH** for 6 minutes per pound. Glaze with preserves after half of the cooking period.

My cooking time: ☐

Braised Chicken

TOTAL COOKING TIME: 27 minutes
Serves 6
3-quart glass casserole dish

2 whole frying chickens size pieces
1 bottle (12-ounces) dark beer
1 cup light cream
1 pound mushrooms, sliced
1 onion, sliced
Salt and pepper
½ cup flour

Place chickens in glass casserole. Cover with wax paper, cook on **HIGH** for 10 minutes. Add remaining ingredients, except flour. Cook, uncovered on **HIGH** 10 to 12 minutes longer. Remove chicken from sauce to serving platter. Mix flour with enough water to make a paste. Stir into sauce. Cook on **HIGH** for 5 minutes or until thickened. Pour sauce over chicken.

My cooking time: ☐

◄*Onion and Cheese Chicken Bake*

Almond Chicken

TOTAL COOKING TIME: 10 minutes
Serves 4
9-inch square glass baking dish

4 chicken breasts, skinned and boned (about 1½ pounds after boning)
4 slices bacon
½ teaspoon *each* seasoned salt and pepper
1 can (10¾-ounces) condensed cream of onion soup
¼ cup dry sherry
¼ cup sliced almonds, toasted

Wrap each chicken breast with bacon slice and season. Arrange in baking dish; cover with wax paper. Cook on **HIGH** for 4 to 5 minutes. Combine soup and wine, pour over chicken. Continue to cook, uncovered on **HIGH** for 4 to 5 minutes. Allow to stand 5 minutes; top with almonds before serving.

My cooking time: ☐

TIP: To toast nuts, spread ¼ cup nuts in glass pie plate. Cook on **HIGH** for 3 to 3½ minutes, stirring frequently, until golden.

Spanish Chicken and Rice

TOTAL COOKING TIME: 30 minutes
Serves 4
3-quart glass casserole dish

2½ to 3 pounds frying chicken, cut in serving size pieces
1 cup uncooked rice
1 package (1¼-ounce) Spanish rice mix
1½ cups water
½ cup sherry
¼ cup chopped onion
1 teaspoon salt

In glass casserole, combine all ingredients. Cover; cook on **HIGH** for 20 minutes; turn chicken pieces and cook on **MED/DEF** for 10 minutes longer or until chicken and rice are tender.

My cooking time: ☐

Polynesian Chicken

TOTAL COOKING TIME: 22 minutes
Serves 4 to 6
12 x 7½-inch glass baking dish

2 to 3 pounds frying chicken, cut in serving size pieces
1 can (6-ounces) orange juice concentrate
1 tablespoon cornstarch
1 tablespoon lime juice
1 teaspoon salt
¼ teaspoon cinnamon
3 bananas, peeled and sliced
½ cup chopped macadamia nuts
½ cup coconut, toasted

Arrange chicken in glass baking dish skin side down with meatiest pieces toward outside. Cover with wax paper, cook on **HIGH** for 10 minutes. Turn pieces over. Mix juice concentrate, cornstarch, lime juice, salt, and cinnamon. Pour over chicken, continue to cook on **HIGH** for 10 to 12 minutes. Add bananas and nuts, cover with wax paper. Let stand 5 minutes before serving. Garnish with toasted coconut.

My cooking time: ☐

TIP: To toast coconut, spread in glass pie plate. Cook on **HIGH** for 6 minutes or until golden, stirring frequently.

◄ Almond Chicken

Chicken Avocado

TOTAL COOKING TIME: 14 minutes
Serves 6
12 x 7½-inch glass baking dish

- 6 chicken breasts, skinned and boned (about 2 pounds after boning)
- 4 tablespoons butter
- 1 tablespoon soy sauce
- ½ cup pineapple juice
- ½ teaspoon powdered ginger
- 4 cups hot cooked rice
- 2 ripe avocados, sliced
- 1½ teaspoons cornstarch
- Dash paprika, if desired

In glass baking dish combine butter, soy sauce, pineapple juice, and ginger. Cook on **MED/DEF** for 3 minutes, or until mixture bubbles. Roll chicken pieces in sauce to coat and arrange in dish. Cover with wax paper. Cook on **HIGH** for 6 minutes. Turn pieces over, and continue to cook 6 to 8 minutes. Remove chicken from dish, reserving juices. Arrange cooked chicken on platter over cooked rice; top with avocado slices. In glass mixing bowl, stir 1 cup reserved juices into cornstarch. Cook on **HIGH** for 1 to 2 minutes or until sauce is thick and clear. Pour sauce over chicken, avocado and rice platter. Sprinkle with paprika if desired.

My cooking time: ☐

Chicken Marengo

TOTAL COOKING TIME: 22 minutes
Serves 4 to 6
13 x 9-inch glass baking dish

- 2½ to 3 pounds frying chicken, cut in serving size pieces
- 1 package (1½-ounces) spaghetti sauce mix
- 1 can (14½-ounces) whole tomatoes
- ¼ cup sauterne wine
- ½ pound fresh mushrooms, sliced

In glass measuring cup combine spaghetti sauce mix, tomatoes and wine. Cook on **HIGH** for 5 minutes to combine flavors. Set aside. Arrange chicken in baking dish skin side down, meatiest pieces toward outside. Cover with wax paper, cook on **HIGH** for 10 minutes. Turn pieces over, top with sliced mushrooms. Pour sauce over chicken. Continue to cook covered on **HIGH** for 10 to 12 minutes. Let stand for 5 minutes before serving.

My cooking time: ☐

Cranberry Chicken

TOTAL COOKING TIME: 22 minutes
Serves 4 to 6
13 x 9-inch glass baking dish
4 cup glass measuring cup

- **2½ to 3 pounds frying chicken, cut in serving size pieces**
- **Salt and pepper to taste**
- **1 can (16-ounces) whole cranberry sauce**
- **1 tablespoon sugar**
- **1 tablespoon lemon juice**
- **2 tablespoons butter**
- **¼ teaspoon *each* ground cloves and cinnamon**

In large glass measuring cup, combine cranberry sauce, sugar, lemon juice, butter and spices. Cook on **MED/DEF** for 2 to 3 minutes or until butter melts. Set aside. Season chicken pieces with salt and pepper. Arrange in glass baking dish skin side down with meatiest pieces toward the outside. Cover with wax paper, cook on **HIGH** for 10 minutes. Turn pieces over, spoon prepared sauce over chicken. Cook, uncovered, on **HIGH** for 10 to 12 minutes or until chicken is fork tender. Let stand 5 minutes before serving.

My cooking time: ☐

◄*Chicken Avocado*

Microbaked Chicken

TOTAL COOKING TIME: 22 to 24 minutes
Serves 4 to 6
13 x 9-inch glass baking dish

2½ to 3 pounds frying chicken, cut in serving size pieces
1 package (3¾-ounces) seasoned coating mix for chicken
Dash paprika, if desired

Coat chicken with seasoned mix as instructed on package. Arrange chicken in baking dish skin side down, with meatiest portions toward outside of dish. Cover with wax paper. Cook on **HIGH** for 12 minutes. Turn pieces over; continue to cook, covered on **HIGH** for 10 to 12 minutes, or until pieces are fork tender. Allow to stand 5 minutes before serving. Sprinkle paprika, if desired.

My cooking time: ☐

Teriyaki Chicken

TOTAL COOKING TIME: 22 minutes
Serves 4 to 6
13 x 9-inch glass baking dish
1 cup glass measuring cup

2½ to 3 pounds frying chicken, cut in serving size pieces
⅓ cup soy sauce
2 tablespoons sugar
2 tablespoons dry sherry
¼ teaspoon ground ginger
2 cloves garlic, minced or pressed
1½ teaspoons cornstarch
1 can (8-ounces) bamboo shoots, drained
1 can (8-ounces) water chestnuts, drained and sliced

In glass measuring cup combine soy sauce, sugar, sherry, garlic, cornstarch and ginger. Cook on **HIGH** for 1½ to 2 minutes, or until bubbly and clear, stirring frequently. Set aside. Arrange chicken pieces in glass baking dish, skin side down, meatiest pieces toward outside. Cover with wax paper, cook on **HIGH** for 10 minutes. Turn pieces over, pour sauce over chicken. Continue to cook, uncovered on **HIGH** for 8 to 10 minutes, adding bamboo shoots and water chestnuts during last 2 minutes of cooking period. Allow to stand 5 minutes before serving.

My cooking time: ☐

Stuffed Chicken Breasts

TOTAL COOKING TIME: 20 minutes
Serves 6
12 x 7½-inch glass baking dish
4 cup glass measuring cup

6 chicken breasts, skinned and boned
¼ cup dry sherry
1 box (6-ounces) chicken flavored stuffing mix
¼ cup butter
1 jar (14½-ounces) artichoke hearts, drained
3 pieces bacon, cooked and crumbled

CREAM SAUCE
2 tablespoons butter
2 tablespoons flour
1 cup milk
1 tablespoon dry sherry

Arrange chicken in glass baking dish, add sherry. Cover with wax paper, cook on **HIGH** for 6 minutes. Turn pieces over, continue to cook for 6 minutes or until fork tender. Remove chicken from baking dish. Drain juices into measuring cup. Add water if necessary, until liquid totals 1 cup. Combine juices with seasoning packet from stuffing mix and butter in large glass measuring cup. Cook on **MED/DEF** for 5 minutes. Stir in stuffing crumbs, mixing lightly. Spoon 2/3 of prepared stuffing in bottom of original baking dish, or attractive serving platter. Place cooked chicken over stuffing. Arrange artichoke hearts around chicken pieces. Top with remaining stuffing. Sprinkle on bacon. Pour cream sauce over top. Return to oven to heat through if necessary.

My cooking time: ☐

TIP: To make cream sauce: Melt butter in glass measuring cup; stir in flour and gradually add milk and sherry, stirring well. Cook on **HIGH** for 3 to 4 minutes stirring twice.

◄ *Microbaked Chicken.*

Chicken with Mushrooms and Wine

TOTAL COOKING TIME: 20 to 22 minutes
Serves 4 to 6
13 x 9-inch glass baking dish

2½ to 3 pounds frying chicken, cut in serving size pieces
1 teaspoon *each* seasoned salt and pepper
2 can (10¾-ounces each) condensed golden mushroom soup
½ cup dry sherry
½ pound fresh mushrooms, sliced

Arrange chicken in baking dish skin side down, with meatiest pieces toward outside of dish. Sprinkle with seasonings. Cover dish with wax paper. Cook on **HIGH** for 10 minutes. Turn pieces over. Combine soup, wine, and mushrooms; pour over chicken. Continue to cook, uncovered on **HIGH** for 10 to 12 minutes or until chicken is fork tender. Cover with wax paper and allow to stand 5 minutes before serving.

My cooking time: ☐

Orange Chicken

TOTAL COOKING TIME: 25 minutes
Serves 4
3-quart glass casserole dish

2½ to 3 pounds frying chicken, cut in serving size pieces
1 cup orange juice
½ cup chili sauce
1 tablespoon brown sugar
1 tablespoon soy sauce
½ teaspoon prepared mustard
¼ teaspoon liquid garlic juice
2 tablespoons cornstarch

Arrange chicken pieces in glass casserole, skin side down, meatiest pieces towards outside. Cover with wax paper. Cook on **HIGH** for 10 minutes. Turn chicken pieces over. Combine remaining ingredients except cornstarch and pour over chicken. Cook, uncovered on **HIGH** 10 to 12 minutes. Remove chicken from sauce to serving platter. Combine cornstarch with enough liquid to make a paste. Mix into sauce and cook on **HIGH** for 3 minutes or until thickened. Pour sauce over chicken.

My cooking time: ☐

Chicken and Dumplings

TOTAL COOKING TIME: 31 minutes
Serves 4 to 6
4-quart glass casserole dish

2½ to 3 pounds frying chicken, cut in serving size pieces
2 stalks celery, cut into 1-inch pieces
1 medium onion, sliced
4 carrots, cut into thin slices
1 tablespoon seasoned salt
1 can (10¾-ounces) condensed cream of chicken soup
1 can (10¾-ounces) condensed chicken broth

DUMPLINGS
2 cups biscuit mix
⅔ cup milk
1 tablespoon chopped parsley
1 tablespoon Parmesan cheese

In glass casserole, combine chicken, celery, onion, carrots, seasoning and soups. Cover; cook on **HIGH** for 25 minutes, stirring occasionally. Meanwhile, prepare dumplings. Spoon dumplings around outside edge of casserole. Cook on **HIGH**, uncovered for 6 minutes.

My cooking time: ☐

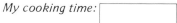

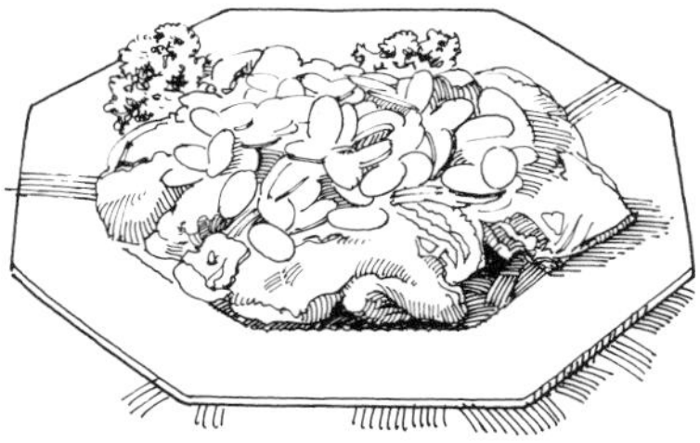

◀ *Chicken with Mushrooms and Wine.*

Easy Curried Chicken

TOTAL COOKING TIME: 22 minutes
Serves 4
3-quart glass casserole dish

2½ to 3 pounds frying chicken, cut in serving size pieces
1 can (10¾-ounces) condensed cream of chicken soup
1 can (8-ounces) crushed pineapple, drained
½ cup raisins (optional)
1 tablespoon curry powder

Arrange chicken pieces in glass casserole, skin side down, meatiest pieces towards outside. Cover with wax paper, cook on **HIGH** for 10 minutes. Turn chicken pieces over. Combine remaining ingredients and pour over chicken. Cook, uncovered on **HIGH** for 10 to 12 minutes longer.

My cooking time:

Chicken Cacciatore

TOTAL COOKING TIME: 30 minutes
Serves 4
3-quart covered glass casserole dish

2½ to 3 pounds frying chicken, cut in serving size pieces
1 can (16-ounces) whole tomatoes
1 teaspoon salt
1 teaspoon oregano
1 bay leaf
1 clove garlic, pressed or chopped

In glass casserole, combine all ingredients. Cover; cook on **HIGH** for 20 minutes, then **MED/DEF** for 10 minutes.

My cooking time:

Chicken Fricassee

TOTAL COOKING TIME: 32 minutes
Serves 4
3-quart covered glass casserole dish

6 slices bacon
2½ to 3 pounds frying chicken, cut in serving size pieces
6 carrots, cut in 1 inch pieces
1½ cups water
2 chicken bouillon cubes
1 tablespoon chopped parsley
1 teaspoon salt
½ cup light cream
½ cup flour
2 egg yolks, lightly beaten

Place bacon between layers of paper towels and cook on **HIGH** for 6 minutes or until crisp. Place chicken pieces in glass casserole. Crumble bacon and add to chicken along with water, bouillon, parsley and salt. Cover; cook on **HIGH** for 20 minutes, then on **MED/DEF** for 10 minutes or until chicken is tender. Remove chicken from sauce to serving platter. Combine light cream and flour; thoroughly mix into chicken drippings. Cook on **MED/DEF** for 5 minutes. Stir ¼ cup hot mixture into yolks, then add to sauce and cook on **MED/DEF** for 2 minutes. Pour sauce over chicken and serve.

My cooking time:

Seafood

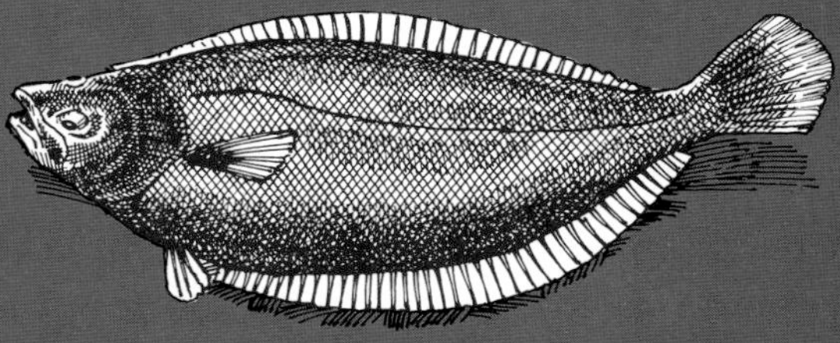

Both fish and shellfish cook beautifully in the microwave oven. Seafood is done in minutes and retains its moist fresh flavor. With microwave cooking, there is no need to use oil or butter so naturally low calorie fish is even better for the diet conscious.

As a General Rule:

- Cook covered.
- Cook on power level **HIGH**.
- Make sure frozen seafood is completely thawed before cooking. Be sure all excess liquid is drained before cooking.
- Arrange fish evenly in dish with smaller or thinner ends toward the center of dish.
- Cook fish until just firm and it flakes easily.

Approximate Cooking Time:
- 5 minutes per pound for steaks or fillets
- 7 minutes per pound for whole fish
- 4 minutes per pound for shellfish

Microwave Method: Fish

The method below is for fish that is thoroughly thawed. Remember to cook only until the fish loses its transparent color and flakes easily with a fork.

1. In glass dish melt enough butter if desired to coat bottom. A 9" X 9" square or 9" X 13 " oblong dish is recommended depending on quantity of fish being cooked.
2. Place fully defrosted fish in dish with smaller or less thick ends towards the center. Fish should be equally distributed throughout the dish.
3. Cook on power level **HIGH** until fish is opaque in appearance and flakes easily. If necessary, rotate the dish during cooking time. The time depends on amount of fish. A good rule is approximately 5 minutes per pound for fish steaks or fillets and whole fish will require about 7 minutes per pound. Do no overcook or fish will become tough and dry.
4. If using a sauce, add it before cooking the fish for time given above.

TIPS: Unless called for in a sauce, add lemon juice to fish at the end of cooking. This will help keep the fish from becoming mushy.
If fish fillet is thicker on one side, fold thin side under for more even cooking.

Microwave Method: Shellfish

Shellfish can be cooked in or out of the shell using the following method:

LOBSTER:

1. Place lobster tails, which have been thoroughly thawed, in a glass dish meat side up. If tails won't lie flat, cut lengthwise down the back shell and press until flat.
2. Brush with melted butter and cover.
3. Cook on power level **HIGH** until lobster loses its transparent color. Lobster will require about 4 to 5 minutes per pound. Be careful not to over-cook it.
4. Lobster is now ready to be served or chilled for use in a salad.

SHRIMP OR CRAB LEGS:

1. Shell and devein thawed shrimp or wash crab legs.
2. Place in glass dish and cover.
3. Cook on power level **HIGH** until shrimp is pink. It will take about 3 to 4 minutes per pound.
4. It is now ready to be combined with a sauce or chilled to serve with a salad.

Tips for Defrosting Fish

- For quick, even defrosting always cover fish.
- Always defrost fish on Power Level **DEFROST** to avoid cooking.
- Always drain all excess water from defrosted fish and blot with paper towels.

My Notes:

Bouillabaise

TOTAL COOKING TIME: 25 minutes
Serves 4 to 6
4-quart glass bowl

12 clams in shell
1 pound crab in shell, cut into small chunks
1 pound firm fleshed fish, cut into bite-size chunks
1 pound jumbo shrimp in shell
2 cans (16-ounces each) stewed tomatoes
2 bottles (8-ounces each) clam juice
1 green pepper, cut into chunks
2 stalks celery, cut into chunks

Rinse all fish well. Place into glass bowl. Add remaining ingredients plus water, if necessary to cover fish. Cover; cook on **HIGH** for 25 minutes, stirring every five minutes.

My cooking time:

TIP: Great served with French bread.

Shrimp Creole

TOTAL COOKING TIME: 13 minutes
Serves 4
2-quart glass casserole dish

3 tablespoons butter
½ cup diced onion
½ cup diced green pepper
½ cup diced celery
2 cloves garlic, chopped or pressed
1 tablespoon cornstarch
1 can (16-ounces) stewed tomatoes, chopped
1 can (8-ounces) tomato sauce
1 tablespoon Worcestershire sauce
1 teaspoon chili powder
Dash Tabasco
1 pound cooked bay shrimp
Hot cooked rice

In glass casserole, cook butter on **HIGH** for 1¼ minutes or until melted. Add onion, green pepper, celery and garlic. Cover; cook on **HIGH** for 2 minutes or until vegetables are tender. Mix in cornstarch. Stir well. Add remaining ingredients except shrimp and rice. Cook on **HIGH** for 5 minutes or until bubbling; stir twice during cooking. Add shrimp. Cook on **HIGH** for 4 minutes or until hot. Serve over rice.

My cooking time:

Texas Crab Brunch

TOTAL COOKING TIME: 13 minutes
Serves 4
1-quart glass measuring cup
13 x 9-inch glass baking dish

2 tablespoons butter
2 tablespoons flour
2 cups milk
1 cup grated Cheddar cheese
1 teaspoon prepared mustard
1 egg, slightly beaten
2 cans (6½-ounces each) crab meat
½ teaspoon Worcestershire sauce
Dash Tabasco
Salt to taste
4 English muffins, split and toasted
¼ cup toasted bread crumbs

In glass measuring cup, cook butter on **HIGH** for 45 seconds or until melted. Mix in flour and milk. Stir well. Cook on **HIGH** for 6 to 7 minutes or until thickened. Stir in cheese, mustard, egg, crab meat, Worcestershire sauce, Tabasco and salt. Place toasted English muffins in glass baking dish. Spoon mixture on top. Sprinkle with bread crumbs. Cook on **HIGH** for 5 minutes, or until hot.

My cooking time:

◄ *Bouillabaise*

Qualitätswein
mit Prädikat
Anbaugebiet
NAHE
Burg Layen
bei Bingen a.Rh.

Chinese Shrimp

TOTAL COOKING TIME: 14 minutes
Serves 4
2-quart glass casserole dish

½ pound fresh Chinese pea pods
1 cup chopped green onions
1 cup sliced mushrooms
1 cup sliced celery
½ cup water
1 cube chicken boullion
½ cup roasted cashew nuts
1 teaspoon cornstarch
1 teaspoon salt
½ pound cooked shrimp

In glass casserole, cook water, boullion, cornstarch and salt on **HIGH** for 4 minutes or until thick. Add all remaining ingredients except shrimp. Cover; cook on **HIGH** for 5 minutes or until vegetables are just crisp. Add shrimp, cover, cook on **HIGH** for 3 to 5 minutes or until hot.

My cooking time: ______

Frozen Lobster Tails

TOTAL COOKING TIME: 10 minutes
Serves 4
7 x 3-inch glass baking dish
Glass custard cup

2 cups frozen cooked lobster tails (about 7 to 8-ounces each)
½ cup butter
2 shallots, diced
2 cloves garlic, chopped or pressed
1 tablespoon lemon juice

To thaw lobster tails, place in glass baking dish; cover and cook on **MED/DEF** for 5 minutes. Let sit for 5 minutes or until thawing is complete; then carefully slit shell lengthwise down the middle and pry open with fingers. Carefully grasp end of meat, pull out in one piece and place on top of shell. In glass custard cup, cook butter on HIGH for 1½ minutes. Add shallots and garlic. Cook on **HIGH** for 1 minute, then add lemon juice. Place lobster tails in baking dish and pour butter mixture on top. Cover; cook on **HIGH** for 2 minutes or until opaque. Let stand to complete cooking. Overcooking causes lobster to toughen. Strain butter and serve as accompaniment.

My cooking time: ______

Sole Amandine

TOTAL COOKING TIME: 16 minutes
Serves 4
11 x 7-inch glass baking dish

6 tablespoons butter
¾ cup (3-ounce package) slivered almonds
1 pound sole fillets
1 tablespoon chopped parsley
Salt and pepper to taste
1 tablespoon lemon juice

In baking dish, cook butter on **HIGH** for 1½ minutes, or until melted. Stir in almonds. Cook on **HIGH** for 6 minutes, or until almonds are golden brown, stirring twice during cooking. Add fish fillets and parsley. Cover; cook on **HIGH** for 6 to 8 minutes, or until fish can be flaked with a fork; turn dish once during cooking. Sprinkle with lemon juice and season as desired with salt and pepper.

My cooking time: ______

◄ *Sole Amandine*

Lobster Thermidor

TOTAL COOKING TIME: 14 minutes
Serves 4
1½-quart glass casserole dish

¼ cup butter
2 cups sliced fresh mushrooms
¼ cup chopped green onions
2 tablespoons flour
2 cups light cream
1 teaspoon salt
½ teaspoon garlic powder
¼ teaspoon dry mustard
2 cups bite-size cooked lobster chunks
¼ cup Parmesan cheese
1 tablespoon sherry
¼ cup bread crumbs

In glass casserole, cook butter on **HIGH** for 1¼ minutes or until melted. Stir in mushrooms and onion. Cook on **HIGH** for 2 minutes or until tender. Stir in flour; add cream, salt, garlic and mustard, stirring well. Cook on **HIGH** for 4 minutes, or until thick; stir once during cooking. Mix in lobster, Parmesan cheese and sherry. Top with bread crumbs. Cover; cook on **HIGH** for 4 minutes or until hot. Serve over rice.

My cooking time: ______

Shrimp Stuffed Sole

TOTAL COOKING TIME: 11 minutes
Serves 4
8-inch square glass baking dish

6 tablespoons butter, divided
1 can (4½-ounces) shrimp, drained and chopped
½ cup bread crumbs
¼ cup light cream
1 tablespoon chopped parsley
1 pound sole fillets
1 teaspoon dill weed
1 teaspoon paprika
Salt to taste
2 tablespoons lemon juice

In glass bowl, cook 3 tablespoons butter on **HIGH** for 1¼ minutes or until melted. Mix in shrimp, bread crumbs, cream and parsley. Set aside. In glass baking dish, cook remaining 3 tablespoons butter on **HIGH** for 1¼ minutes or until melted. Cut fillets in half lengthwise and place in melted butter. Spoon even amount of shrimp mixture onto each fillet half. Fold each end toward center so both ends are tucked under. Sprinkle with dill weed and paprika. Cook on **HIGH** for 6 to 8 minutes or until fish can be flaked with a fork. Sprinkle with lemon juice and salt to taste.

My cooking time: ______

Oriental Sole

TOTAL COOKING TIME: 8 minutes
Serves 4
11 x 7-inch glass baking dish

2 tablespoons soy sauce
2 tablespoons lemon juice
1 tablespoon catsup
½ teaspoon ground ginger
1 pound sole fillets
1 orange, sliced thin
Salt to taste

In glass baking dish, combine soy sauce, lemon juice, catsup and ginger. Place sole fillets in mixture turning fillets over to coat. Place orange slices evenly over fish. Cover; cook on **HIGH** for 6 to 8 minutes or until fish flakes with a fork; turn dish once during cooking.

My cooking time: ______

◄*Shrimp Stuffed Sole*

Crepes St. Jacques

TOTAL COOKING TIME: 12 minutes
Makes 6 large crepes
2-quart glass bowl
1-quart glass bowl
13 x 9-inch glass baking dish

5 tablespoons butter, divided
¼ pound fresh mushrooms, sliced
2 medium cloves garlic, chopped or pressed
2 tablespoons lemon juice
1 pound scallops, cut into bite size pieces
2 tablespoons flour
Dash pepper
1½ cups light cream
½ cup dry sherry
Parsley flakes to garnish
6 crepes

In large glass mixing bowl, melt 3 tablespoons butter on **HIGH** for 1¼ minutes. Add mushrooms, garlic and lemon juice. Cook on **HIGH** for 2 minutes or until mushrooms are tender. Mix in scallops. Cook on **HIGH** for 2 minutes. Set aside. To make white sauce, in smaller glass mixing bowl, melt remaining 2 tablespoons butter on **HIGH** for 1 minute. Mix in flour and cream. Cook on **HIGH** for 4 to 5 minutes, or until thick; stir once during cooking. Add sherry and season with pepper. Pour ¾ cup white sauce into scallop and mushroom mixture. Fill crepes with scallop mushroom mixture. Fold each crepe into thirds and place into glass baking dish. Pour remaining sauce on top. Cover; cook on **HIGH** for 2 minutes or until hot. Garnish with parsley.

My cooking time: ☐

Halibut in Lemon Sauce

TOTAL COOKING TIME: 10 minutes
Serves 4
2-cup glass bowl
9-inch square glass baking dish

3 tablespoons butter
3 tablespoons chopped onion
1 tablespoon chopped parsley
2 teaspoons lemon juice
½ teaspoon prepared mustard
½ teaspoon garlic powder
1½ pounds halibut fillets

In glass bowl, cook butter on **HIGH** for 1¼ minutes, or until melted. Add onion, parsley, lemon juice, mustard and garlic powder. Mix well. Arrange fillets in glass baking dish with smallest portion towards center. Top with butter mixture. Cover; cook on **HIGH** for 6 to 8 minutes or until fish flakes with a fork.

My cooking time: ☐

Salmon with Broccoli

TOTAL COOKING TIME: 15 minutes
Serves 4
2-quart glass casserole dish

1 package (10-ounces) frozen broccoli spears
2 tablespoons butter
1 pound salmon fillets
1 can (10-ounces) condensed cream of shrimp soup
½ teaspoon tarragon
¼ teaspoon dill weed
Salt to taste

In original package, with outer wrapper removed, cook broccoli on **HIGH** for 3 minutes. Open package and separate stalks to help dissolve ice crystals. Continue cooking on **HIGH** for 2 minutes or until heated. Set aside. In glass baking dish, arrange salmon fillets with smallest portions towards the center of dish. Sprinkle with lemon juice and dot with butter. Cover; cook on **HIGH** for 5 minutes or until fish flakes with a fork. Arrange broccoli on top of fish with spears towards the center. Pour soup over broccoli. Sprinkle with tarragon and dill weed. Cover; cook on **HIGH** for 5 minutes, or until hot.

My cooking time: ☐

◄*Salmon with Broccoli*

Washington Stuffed Trout

TOTAL COOKING TIME: 8 minutes
Serves 4
13 x 9-inch glass baking dish

8 slices bacon, divided
1 cup cooked rice
¼ cup raisins
1 tablespoon chopped parsley
1 teaspoon lemon juice
4 whole trout, deboned

In glass baking dish, cook 4 slices bacon on **HIGH** for 3 minutes or until crisp. Drain. Chop bacon and combine with rice, raisins, parsley and lemon juice. Fill each trout cavity with an equal portion of filling. Wrap one slice bacon around each stuffed trout and place in glass baking dish. Cook on **HIGH** for 5 minutes or until done.

My cooking time:

TIP: For crisper bacon on outside, partially cook bacon before wrapping.

Company Salmon

TOTAL COOKING TIME: 10 minutes
Serves 4
11 x 9-inch glass baking dish

4 tablespoons butter
½ cup toasted bread crumbs
½ cup chopped celery
½ cup sliced mushrooms
¼ cup light cream
¼ cup chopped onion
2 tablespoons lemon juice
4 salmon steaks (about 2 pounds)

In glass mixing bowl, cook butter on **HIGH** for 1¼ minutes, or until melted. Add remaining ingredients, except salmon. Arrange salmon in glass baking dish, smallest portion towards center. Top with butter mixture. Cover; cook on **HIGH** for 7 to 9 minutes, or until fish flakes with a fork, turning dish once during cooking.

My cooking time:

Salmon Quiche

TOTAL COOKING TIME: 20 minutes
Serves 4 to 6
9-inch glass pie dish

2 cans (7¾-ounces each) salmon
⅔ cup sliced stuffed green olives
2 tablespoons chopped parsley
1 9-inch baked pastry shell
1 cup grated Cheddar cheese
2 tablespoons chopped onion
3 eggs slightly beaten
1 cup milk
½ teaspoon salt

In medium bowl, combine salmon, olives and parsley. Place mixture in baked pastry shell and sprinkle with grated Cheddar cheese. Combine milk, eggs, onion and salt. Mix well. Pour over salmon mixture. Cook on **MED/DEF** for 18 to 20 minutes; turn dish twice during cooking. Let sit for 10 minutes or until center is firm.

My cooking time:

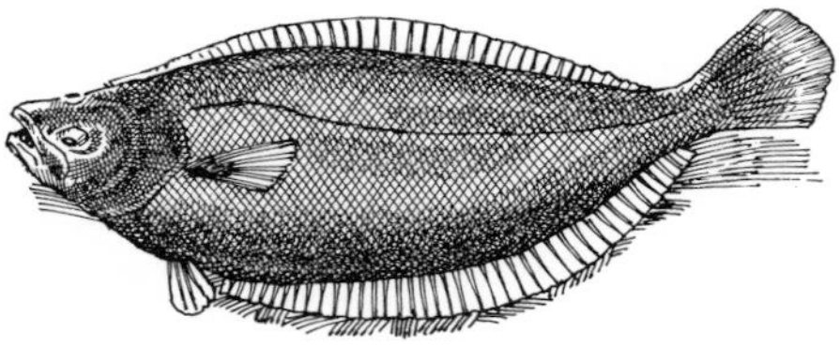

Eggs & Cheese

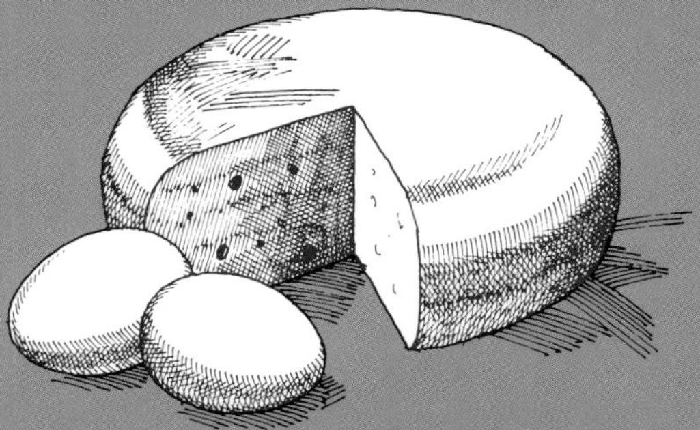

Microwaves work magic with eggs. Scrambling, hard cooking or poaching eggs are easy to do and require much less time and watching. Scrambled eggs are lighter, fluffier and have greater volume. Hard cooked eggs are done in minutes in a dish rather than in the shell. Cheese melts quickly and smoothly. When serving cheese as an appetizer it's flavor is at a peak when served at room temperature. Pop it in the oven for a minute and it goes from refrigerated to ready to serve whenever unexpected company drops in.

As a General Rule: Eggs

- Never cook eggs in the shell.
- Cook on power level **MED/DEF** for best results.
- Alway pierce the yolk with a toothpick when baking, poaching or hard cooking. (Pressure within the yolk as it cooks could cause it to explode).
- Buttering dish before cooking the eggs will make the dish easier to clean.

Microwave Method: Eggs

To Scramble:

1. Mix as desired and place in any buttered microwave suitable dish.
2. Cook on **MED/DEF** until done. Stir as necessary. (The more eggs the more stirring required to bring the uncooked egg to outer part of dish). Cook **about 45 seconds per egg.**

To Bake or Hard Cook:

1. Place egg in buttered dish. Custard cup (6-ounces) or paper cup.
2. Always pierce yolk with toothpick.
3. Cover with plastic wrap.
4. Cook on **MED/DEF** until done as desired. Allow about 30 seconds per egg for soft center, 45 seconds for hard center. (For soft center remove before whites are completely set. Allow for standing time to finish cooking).

To Poach:

1. In a 6-ounce custard cup, heat ¼ cup water until boiling, ¼ teaspoon vinegar may be added, if desired.
2. Place egg into boiling water.
3. Always pierce yolk.
4. Cover with plastic wrap.
5. Cook on **MED/DEF** until done as desired. Each egg will take about 1 minute.

As a General Rule: Cheese

- Use, power level **MED/DEF** for melting.
- Cheese melts best when grated and combined with milk or other liquids.

TIPS: **Softening dairy products:**
To soften butter, cream cheese, or ice cream for serving or using in a recipe, heat on **MED/DEF** for 15 to 30 seconds, or until soft.

Melting Butter:
Heat On **HIGH** until melted.

Clarified Butter:
Let butter boil and then stand for 1 minute. Clear butter on top may then be poured off for use.

My Notes:

Welsh Rarebit

TOTAL COOKING TIME: 13 minutes
Makes 4 cups
2-quart glass casserole dish

1 pound Cheddar cheese, grated (about 4 cups)
½ cup beer
1 teaspoon seasoned salt
1 teaspoon Worcestershire sauce
½ teaspoon dry mustard
2 eggs, slightly beaten
Paprika
Crusty French bread

Combine cheese, beer, salt, Worcesterhsire, and dry mustard in glass casserole. Cook on **MED/DEF** for 8 to 9 minutes or until cheese blends easily into mixture. Add eggs gradually to prevent curdling. Cook on **MED/DEF** for 3 to 4 minutes or until mixture thickens. Sprinkle with paprika. Serve over bread slices or cubes.

My cooking time: ☐

Cheese Omelet

TOTAL COOKING TIME: 8 minutes
Serves 2
9-inch glass pie plate

4 eggs
¼ cup light cream
½ teaspoon seasoned salt and pepper
¼ teaspoon baking powder
2 tablespoons butter
½ cup grated Cheddar cheese

Beat eggs, cream, seasonings, and baking powder until well blended. Place butter in glass pie plate. Cook on **HIGH** for 1 minute or until melted. Pour egg mixture into hot butter. Cook on **MED/DEF** for 6 to 8 minutes or until center is almost set. Sprinkle with grated cheese. Fold in half and serve.

My cooking time: ☐

Quiche Lorraine

TOTAL COOKING TIME: 28 minutes
Serves 6
9-inch pie plate

4 slices bacon, cooked and crumbled
1 9-inch pastry shell
1 cup grated Swiss cheese
¼ cup chopped green onion
3 eggs
1 cup light cream
½ teaspoon fines herbs

Pierce pastry shell. Cook on **HIGH** for 4 to 5 minutes or just until brown spots begin to appear. Sprinkle baked crust with cheese and onion. In small bowl beat eggs; add cream and seasonings. Pour eggs and cream into crust. Sprinkle bacon on top of quiche. Cook on **MED/DEF** for 15 to 20 minutes or until center is firm.

My cooking time: ☐

QUICHE VARIATIONS:

Chili-Onion Quiche

Follow the recipe for Quiche Lorraine (above) substituting grated Jack cheese for Swiss and diced green chiles for green onion. Sprinkle top of quiche with 1 can (3-ounces) French fried onions.

Sausage and Mushroom Quiche

Follow the recipe for Quiche Lorraine (above) substituting grated Mozzarella cheese for Swiss and 1 cup cooked, crumbled sausage for bacon. Add 1 jar (4-ounces) mushroom stems and pieces, drained, with cheese and onion.

Seafood Quiche

Follow the recipe for Quiche Lorraine (above) substituting ¾ cup chopped cooked shrimp for bacon and ½ teaspoon dried dill weed for fines herbes. Sprinkle top with 1 can (3-ounces) French fried onions if desired.

◄ *Welsh Rarebit*

Scrambled Eggs with Mushrooms

TOTAL COOKING TIME: 8 minutes
Serves 2
1½-quart glass casserole dish

3 slices bacon, cooked and crumbled
4 eggs
¼ cup light cream
2 tablespoons butter
1 can (4-ounces) sliced mushrooms, drained
Dash salt and pepper
Chopped parsley

Beat eggs and cream in glass casserole. Add butter, mushrooms, salt and pepper, and crumbled bacon; stir to blend. Cook on **MED/DEF** for 6 to 8 minutes or until eggs are almost set; stirring twice. Allow to stand to complete cooking. Garnish with chopped parsley.

My cooking time: ☐

Cheese and Crab Fondue

TOTAL COOKING TIME: 9 minutes
Makes 4 cups
1½ quart glass casserole dish

1 can (10¾ ounces) condensed cream of mushroom soup
½ pound natural sharp Cheddar cheese, shredded
½ pound processed sharp Cheddar cheese, cubed
¼ cup dry sherry
3 tablespoons catsup
1 tablespoon Worcestershire sauce
1 tablespoon garlic salt
1 tablespoon diced green chiles
½ pound crab meat

In glass casserole, combine all ingredients except crab. Cook on **MED/DEF** for 6 to 8 minutes, stirring twice, or until cheese is melted. Stir in crab. Cook on **MED/DEF** for 1 minute to heat through. Transfer to a chafing dish with water jacket for serving. Serve with bread cubes or tortilla chips for dipping.

My cooking time: ☐

Seafood Strada

TOTAL COOKING TIME: 37 minutes
Serves 4 to 6
2-quart glass casserole dish

3 cups fresh bread cubes (about 4 slices)
1 can (4½-ounces) shrimp, drained
1 can (6½-ounces) crab, drained
½ cup chopped celery
¼ cup chopped green onions
1 can (10¾-ounces) condensed cream of mushroom soup
2 teaspoons lemon juice
½ teaspoon Worcestershire sauce.
1 cup milk
2 eggs
1 cup shredded Cheddar cheese

Place half of bread cubes in glass casserole dish. Mix seafood, celery, onions, soup, lemon juice, and Worcestershire sauce. Pour over bread cubes. Cover seafood mixture with remaining half of bread cubes. Mix milk and eggs; pour over casserole. Cook on **MED/DEF** for 30 to 35 minutes, turning dish once. Sprinkle with cheese. Cook on **HIGH** for 1 to 2 minutes until cheese is melted.

TIP: This casserole may be assembled the night before; cover with plastic wrap and chill in refrigerator overnight.

My cooking time: ☐

◄ *Scrambled Eggs with Mushrooms*

Basque Eggs

TOTAL COOKING TIME: 9 minutes
Serves 3 to 4
1½-quart glass casserole dish

½ cup diced cooked ham
¼ cup chopped green pepper
1 medium tomato, peeled and diced
2 tablespoons chopped green onion
2 tablespoons chopped celery
¼ cup sliced green olives
1 clove garlic, crushed
2 tablespoons butter
4 eggs, slightly beaten

In glass casserole combine ham, green pepper, tomato, green onion, celery, olives, garlic, and butter. Cook on **HIGH** for 5 minutes, stirring occasionally. Stir in eggs. Cook on **MED/DEF** for 4 minutes, stirring twice.

My cooking time: ______

Chinese Eggs

TOTAL COOKING TIME: 12 minutes
Serves 4
2-quart glass casserole dish

6 eggs
1 can (16-ounces) Chinese vegetables
¼ cup chopped green peppers
2 tablespoons chopped green onions
1 teaspoon soy sauce
2 tablespoons butter

Beat eggs well in glass casserole dish. Add remaining ingredients. Cook on **MED/DEF** for 10 to 12 minutes, stirring twice. Let stand 1 to 2 minutes to complete cooking.

My cooking time: ______

Baked Eggs in Hash

TOTAL COOKING TIME: 6 minutes
Serves 2
2 10-ounce custard cups

1 can (12-ounces) corned beef hash
2 eggs
¼ cup shredded Cheddar cheese
Seasoned salt and pepper

Divide corned beef hash between 2 custard cups. Make a hollow in center of hash with back of spoon. Break 1 egg into each hollow. Pierce yolks with toothpick. Sprinkle each egg with cheese and seasonings. Cover tightly with plastic wrap. Cook on **MED/DEF** for 5 to 6 minutes or until hash is hot and egg white is nearly opaque. Let stand for 1 minute, covered, before serving.

My cooking time: ______

No Fuss Cheese Omelet

TOTAL COOKING TIME: 2½ minutes
Serves 1
8-inch paper plate with heavy edge

1 tablespoon butter
1 egg, beaten
1 tablespoon grated Cheddar cheese

Cook butter on paper plate on **HIGH** for 1 minute. Add beaten egg. Cook on **MED/DEF** for 1½ minutes. About half way through, tip dish to distribute uncooked egg. Place cheese on egg. Loosen edges of omelet. Fold plate in half. Ease omelet out of plate with spatula.

My cooking time: ______

TIP: For fluffier omelet, use a smaller plate.

Fruits

Bake an apple in four minutes or make 2 quarts of strawberry jam in 25 minutes. The baked apple tastes just picked, fresh and flavorful and homemade jam can be served anytime, not just on special occasions. These are just two of the many advantages of cooking fruit the microwave way.

As a General Rule:

- Cook uncovered.
- Cook on power level HIGH.
- Cut into as uniform of pieces as possible.
- Arrange evenly in dish if cooking large pieces of fruit.
- Allow for standing time to finish cooking fruit. Remember to cook only until soft but not mushy.

Microwave Method:

Because there are so many different fruits available we recommend you use the cooking methods in the recipes in this chapter as a guide to cooking fruits.

My Notes:

Apple Betty

TOTAL COOKING TIME: 10 minutes
Serves 6 to 8
2-quart glass baking dish

6 cups sliced apples (about 2 pounds)
1 lemon, grate peel and juice
1/3 cup brown sugar
1/3 cup sugar
1 teaspoon cinnamon
½ teaspoon cardamon
2 cups soft bread crumbs
¼ cup butter, melted

In large bowl, combine apples, lemon peel and juice, sugars, cinnamon, and cardamon. Toss to coat apples with flavorings. Begin layering in baking dish with bread crumbs, alternating with apple mixture. Top off with crumbs. Pour melted butter over top. Cook on **HIGH** for 8 to 10 minutes, or until apples are tender. Serve with cream if desired.

My cooking time: ☐

Baked Apples

TOTAL COOKING TIME: 10 minutes
Serves 4
8-inch round glass baking dish

4 baking apples (Rome Beauty, Pippin, Granny Smith)
Lemon juice
¼ cup brown sugar
¼ cup raisins
¼ cup slivered almonds
1 teaspoon cinnamon
4 teaspoons butter

Core apples. Peel skin from top half of each apple. Arrange apples in baking dish. Sprinkle with lemon juice. Combine sugar, raisins, almonds and cinnamon. Fill centers of each apple with sugar mixture. Dot each apple with butter. Cook on **HIGH** for 8 to 10 minutes or until apples are tender.

My cooking time: ☐

Fruit Compote

TOTAL COOKING TIME: 5 minutes
Serves 4 to 6
1-quart glass casserole dish

1 can (8-ounces) sliced peaches, drained, reserving 2 tablespoons syrup
1 can (8-ounces) apricot halves, drained, reserving 2 tablespoons syrup
¼ teaspoon *each* ground cloves, cinnamon, and allspice
1 can (8-ounces) whole cranberry sauce
2 medium apples, peeled, cored and chunked

In glass casserole dish, stir together syrups and spices. Stir in cranberry sauce and fruits. Cover; cook on **HIGH** for 5 minutes, stirring once. Serve warm or chilled as side dish.

My cooking time: ☐

Cherries and Pears in Wine Sauce

TOTAL COOKING TIME: 6 minutes
Serves 6 to 8
1½-quart glass casserole dish

1 can (16-ounces) dark pitted cherries
1 can (16-ounces) pear halves
¼ cup sweet red wine
1 tablespoon orange peel
2 tablespoons cornstarch

Drain syrup from cherries and pears into glass casserole dish. Stir in wine, orange peel and cornstarch. Cook on **HIGH** for 4 to 6 minutes, or until slightly thickened, stirring twice. Combine fruit with hot sauce. Serve over ice cream or sponge cake.

My cooking time: ☐

Peach Melba

TOTAL COOKING TIME: 6 minutes
Serves 4 to 6
1-quart glass casserole dish

1 can (16-ounces) peach halves
1 package (10-ounces) frozen strawberries, thawed
½ cup currant jelly
1 tablespoon cornstarch

Drain syrup from peaches and strawberries into glass casserole dish. Stir in jelly and cornstarch. Cook on **HIGH** for 4 to 6 minutes, or until slightly thickened, stirring twice. Combine fruit with hot sauce. Serve over ice cream.

My cooking time:

Strawberry Jam

TOTAL COOKING TIME: 25 minutes
Makes 4 pints
2-quart glass measuring bowl

6 cups sliced strawberries
3 cups sugar
¼ cup lemon juice
1 tablespoon lemon peel
2 packages (3-ounces each) strawberry flavored gelatin

In glass measuring bowl, lightly crush berries. Add sugar, lemon juice and peel; let stand for 4 hours. Cook on **HIGH** for 10 to 15 minutes, or until mixture reaches full boil, stirring occasionally. Continue to cook on **MED/DEF** for 10 minutes to simmer gently, stirring occasionally. Remove from oven. Stir in gelatin; let stand 30 minutes. Spoon jam into plastic freezer containers leaving ½-inch space at the top. Let stand until room temperature. Cover withlids. (Jam will thicken when cold). Store in refrigerator or freezer.

My cooking time:

Raspberry Sherbet

TOTAL COOKING TIME: 5 minutes
Makes about 1 quart
2-quart glass mixing bowl

2 cups milk
2 cups miniature marshmallows
1 can (16-ounces) red raspberries, drained, reserving syrup
1 tablespoon lemon juice

In glass mixing bowl, combine milk and marshmallows. Cook on **HIGH** for 5 minutes or until marshmallows melt, stirring twice. Cool quickly in pan of cold water. Add lemon juice to reserved syrup; then slowly add to milk mixture, stirring constantly. Cover bowl with plastic wrap to prevent ice crystal; partially freeze. Beat with mixer at medium speed until smooth and fluffy. Quickly fold in raspberries. Return to freezer to firm.

My cooking time:

Cherries Jubilee

TOTAL COOKING TIME: 6 minutes
Serves 4
1½-quart glass casserole dish

1 can (16-ounces) dark pitted cherries, drained, reserving syrup
¼ cup currant jelly
1 tablespoon cornstarch
¼ cup cherry brandy
Vanilla ice cream

In glass casserole dish combine cherry syrup, jelly, and cornstarch. Cook on **HIGH** for 3 to 4 minutes or until slightly thickened, stirring twice. Add cherries; cook on **HIGH** for 2 minutes to warm. Warm brandy in glass measuring cup on **HIGH** for 30 seconds. Pour over hot cherry sauce. Flame; serve over ice cream.

My cooking time:

◄ *Peach Melba*

Baked Bananas

TOTAL COOKING TIME: 4 minutes
Serves 4
1½-quart glass casserole dish

¼ cup orange juice
1 tablespoon butter
½ teaspoon orange peel
½ teaspoon cinnamon
¼ teaspoon *each* ground cloves and nutmeg
4 bananas, peeled and sliced

In glass casserole dish combine orange juice, butter, orange peel, and spices. Cook on **HIGH** for 2 to 3 minutes or until bubbling, stirring twice. Add bananas. Cook on **HIGH** for 1 minute. Serve warm.

My cooking time:

Bananas Royale

TOTAL COOKING TIME: 5 minutes
Serves 4
1½-quart glass casserole dish

¼ cup butter
¼ cup brown sugar
¼ cup heavy cream
¼ teaspoon cinnamon
¼ teaspoon nutmeg
4 bananas, peeled and sliced
¼ cup brandy
Ice cream

Place butter in glass casserole dish. Cook on **HIGH** for 1½ minutes, or until melted. Stir in sugar, cream, cinnamon and nutmeg. Cook on **HIGH** for 2 minutes. Stir in sliced bananas, turning to coat. Cook on **HIGH** for 2 minutes, stirring once. Warm brandy in glass measuring cup on **HIGH** for 30 seconds. Pour brandy over bananas; flame. Serve over ice cream.

My cooking time:

Stewed Fruit

TOTAL COOKING TIME: 10 minutes
Serves 4 to 6
3-quart covered casserole dish

1 pound mixed dried fruit
½ cup sauterne of white wine
1 cup water

Soak dried fruit in wine for 30 minutes. Add water. Cover; cook on **HIGH** for 10 minutes. Serve hot or cold.

My cooking time:

Holiday Fruit Compote

TOTAL COOKING TIME: 10 minutes
Serves 4 to 6
2-quart covered glass casserole dish

1 cup sugar
¼ cup water
4 cooking apples, sliced
2 cups fresh cranberries
2 cups orange wedges
½ teaspoon each cinnamon and cardamom

In glass casserole, combine water and sugar and cook on **HIGH** for 1 minute or until boiling. Add fruit and spices. Cover, cook on **HIGH** for 10 minutes, or until fruit is tender. Serve hot or cold.

My cooking time:

Vegetables

Sweet tender, juicy flavorful, just picked color are some of the words used to describe microwave cooked vegetables. Never before have you tasted flavor or seen colors like those from a microwave oven. Virtually no water is used, so vegetables retain many of their natural vitamins and a considerable amount of vitamin C.

As a General Rule:

- Cook covered.
- Cook on HIGH
- Only add water to vegetables low in moisture and cut into larger pieces, such as rutabagas, parsnips, carrots and beets. When adding water use no more than ¼ cup.
- Individual vegetables such as artichokes or acorn squash, cook well wrapped individually in plastic wrap.
- Vegetables with skins (all types of potatoes) do not need to be wrapped for cooking, but the skins should be pierced to allow the steam to escape.
- When cutting into pieces, make them as uniform as possible.
- Never add salt before cooking.

Microwave Method:

In the following chart, are directions for preparing many kinds of vegetables. Listed below are the cooking steps.

1. Wash vegetables and cut into desired size, leaving some moisture.
2. Place in covered casserole dish or wrap in plastic wrap. Arrangement in dish or oven is important.
   Remember to:
   - Place larger pieces towards outside of dish.
   - When cooking more than one vegetable in a dish, place the ones which cook the fastest toward the inside.
   - Load the dish as evenly as possible to assure even cooking.
3. Cook for time given in chart on HIGH. Times are for crisp tender doneness. If softer vegetables are desired, cook 1 to 2 additional minutes.
4. Allow to stand several minutes before serving.
5. Salt and serve.

VEGETABLE COOKING CHART

ITEM	QUANTITY	SHAPE	TIME ON POWER LEVEL HIGH (9)	TIPS
Asparagus	1 lb.	whole	10–12 min.	Add ¼ cup water
Artichokes	2 med.	whole	12–15 min.	Wrap individually in plastic wrap
Beans Waxed or Green	1 lb.	2 inch pieces	14–16 min.	Add ¼ cup water
Beets	2 cup	sliced	15 min.	
Broccoli	1 lb.	flowerets	8 min.	
Brussels Sprouts	1 lb.	whole	5–6 min.	
Cabbage	1 head	8 wedges whole	10–12 min. 12–14 min.	Wrap in plastic wrap
Carrots	1 lb. 1 lb.	sliced 2 inch pieces	10 min. 12–14 min.	Add ¼ cup water
Cauliflower	1 head 1½ lb. 1 head	whole pieces	8 min. 8 min.	
Celery	6 stalks	3 inch	8 min.	
Corn	4 ears 2 cups	whole kernels	10 min. 9 min.	Cut off 1 inch stalk from either end. Leave husk and clean after cooking. Silks will fall right off.
Onions	4 med.	whole	9 min.	
Parsnips	1 lb.	3 inch slices	8–9 min.	Add ¼ cup water

ITEM	QUANTITY	SHAPE	TIME ON POWER LEVEL HIGH (9)	TIPS
Peppers, Bell	4 med.	whole	3 min.	
Potatoes				
Baked	2 med. 4 med.		8 min. 14 min.	Pierce skin. Allow to stand 5 min. before serving
Mashed	4 med.	2 inch slices	10 min.	Add ¼ cup water
Red Rose	4 med.	whole	10 min.	Pierce skin
Sweet or Yams	4 med.	whole	8 min.	Pierce skin
Spinach	1 lb.	whole	4 min.	
Squash				
Acorn	1 med.	halfed	8–10 min.	Wrap each half in plastic wrap
Hubbard	2½ lbs.	whole	18 min.	
Summer	1 lb.	quartered	8 min.	
Yellow (crooked neck)	1 lb.	½ inch pieces	10 min.	
Zucchini	1 lb.	½ inch pieces	10 min.	

The following chart gives approximate cooking times for various quantities and package types of vegetables commonly found in the frozen food section of markets. Because these frozen vegetables are in small uniform chunks that easily separate, cooking is fast and even; thus fine results are achieved by cooking them from the frozen state on **HIGH**. Match your package with the instructions below.

FROZEN VEGETABLE COOKING CHART

PACKAGING	WEIGHT	POWER LEVEL	TIME	SPECIAL INSTRUCTIONS
Cook-in-bag	9 to 12 ounces	HIGH	5 to 7 minutes	Pierce bag before cooking. Rearrange vegetables once during cooking.
Regular plastic bag	16 ounces	HIGH	10 to 12 minutes	Place in 1½ quart covered glass casserole. Stir once during cooking.
Cardboard box	7 to 10 ounces	HIGH	6 to 8 minutes	Remove outer wrap. Cook in cardboard box, if desired.
Aluminum tray	10 ounces	HIGH	6 to 8 minutes	Remove from tray and cook in 1½ quart covered casserole. Stir once during cooking.

Creamy Potato Salad

TOTAL COOKING TIME: 16 minutes
Serves 4 to 6
2-quart covered glass casserole dish

4 medium thin skinned potatoes, scrubbed
4 slices uncooked bacon, diced
¾ cup mayonnaise
½ cup diced onion
¼ cup vinegar
¼ cup half and half
2 stalks celery, diced
½ teaspoon pepper

Pierce potatoes several times with fork. Arrange in circle directly on oven tray. Cook on **HIGH** for 10 to 12 minutes, or until slightly soft. Allow to stand and cool. In glass casserole, cook diced bacon on **HIGH** for 3 minutes; do not drain. Add remaining ingredients, except potatoes and mix well. When potatoes are cooled, remove skins, if desired and cut potatoes in half lengthwise, then crosswise into ¼-inch slices. Add sliced potatoes to casserole. Cover; cook on **HIGH** for 4 minutes, or until potatoes are hot.

My cooking time: ☐

TIPS: Some suitable potato varieties are Irish Cobblers, Red Triumps New Potatoes and White Rose.

Boston Baked Beans

TOTAL COOKING TIME: 10 minutes
Serves 6
2-quart covered glass casserole dish

1 can (28-ounces) baked beans
8 slices cooked bacon, crumbled
4 medium tomatoes, diced
1 medium onion, diced
3 tablespoons dark brown sugar

Combine all ingredients in glass casserole dish. Cover; cook on **HIGH** for 10 minutes, or until slightly bubbly; stir twice during cooking.

My cooking time: ☐

Eggplant Italian

TOTAL COOKING TIME: 8 minutes
Serves 4 to 6
2-quart covered glass casserole dish

2 slices uncooked bacon, diced
1 medium green pepper, diced
1 medium garlic clove, chopped or pressed
1 can (8-ounces) tomato sauce
1 medium eggplant, peeled and cut into 1-inch cubes
Salt and pepper to taste
¼ cup grated Parmesan cheese

In glass casserole, cook bacon on **HIGH** for 3 minutes. Do not drain. Add green pepper and garlic. Cook on **HIGH** for 3 minutes, or until green pepper is tender. Add tomato sauce and eggplant. Cover; cook on **HIGH** for 5 minutes, or until eggplant is tender. Add salt and pepper to taste. Sprinkle with Parmesan cheese.

My cooking time: ☐

Healthy Stuffed Zucchini

TOTAL COOKING TIME: 8 minutes
Serves 4
10 x 6 x 1½-inch glass baking dish

2 large zucchini, sliced in half, lengthwise
1 cup sour cream
½ teaspoon garlic powder
¼ cup shredded Jack cheese
2 tablespoons wheat germ

Arrange zucchini in glass baking dish. Cover; cook on **HIGH** for 4 to 6 minutes, or until tender. Scoop cut enough pulp to make a ¼-inch indentation. In mixing bowl, throughly mix sour cream and garlic powder together. Spread evenly onto zucchini halves. Sprinkle with shredded cheese and wheat germ. Cook for 1 to 2 minutes on **HIGH** or until cheese is melted.

My cooking time: ☐

Cole Slaw of a Different Color

TOTAL COOKING TIME: 7 minutes
Serves 6 to 8
3-quart covered glass casserole dish

1 medium head red cabbage, finely chopped (about 4 cups)
2 large tart red apples, diced
½ cup apple cider vinegar
3 tablespoons sugar
3 tablespoons vegetable oil
½ teaspoon salt
¼ teaspoon caraway seeds

In glass casserole, combine all ingredients. Cover, and cook on **HIGH** for 7 to 9 minutes or until cabbage is wilted, but still slightly crisp; stir twice during cooking. Serve hot or cold.

My cooking time: ____

Three Bean Salad

TOTAL COOKING TIME: 7 minutes
Serves 4
1-quart glass serving dish

⅔ cup vinegar
½ cup sugar
1 tablespoon cornstarch
¼ teaspoon pepper
1 medium onion, sliced
1 can (16-ounces) cut green beans, drained
1 can (15-ounces) red kidney beans, drained
1 can (15½-ounces) garbanzo beans, drained

In glass serving dish, combine all ingredients, except beans. Cook on **HIGH** for 3 to 4 minutes, or until mixture thickens and onion is transparent. Toss in beans. Cook on **HIGH** for 3 minutes or until beans are hot.

My cooking time: ____

TIP: To serve cold, chill mixture after beans are added.

Tangy Green Bean Potato Salad

TOTAL COOKING TIME: 14 minutes
Serves 4 to 6
4-quart covered glass casserole dish

4 medium thin skinned potatoes, scrubbed
½ cup salad oil
½ cup vinegar
2 tablespoons sugar
1 medium onion, finely chopped
1 teaspoon salt
1 teaspoon pepper
4 slices cooked bacon, diced
½ pound cooked green beans, cut in 2″ pieces
¼ cup chopped parsley

Pierce potatoes several times with fork. Arrange in circle directly on oven tray. Cook on **HIGH** for 10 to 12 minutes then allow to stand and cool. In glass casserole add oil, vinegar, sugar, onion, salt and pepper. Cover; cook on **HIGH** for 1½ to 2 minutes, or until onion is transparent. When potatoes are cool, remove skins if desired and cut in half lengthwise, then crosswise into ¼-inch slices. Add sliced potatoes and cooked green beans to casserole. Toss gently, so as not to break up potatoes. Sprinkle with parsley. Chill before serving.

My cooking time: ____

◄ *Cole Slaw of a Different Color*

Corn Stuffed Tomatoes

TOTAL COOKING TIME: 4 minutes
Serves 6
9-inch round glass baking dish

6 large firm tomatoes
2 tablespoons grated Parmesan cheese
½ cup seasoned croutons
½ teaspoon garlic powder
¼ teaspoon pepper
1 can (12-ounces) Mexican style corn

In large mixing bowl, combine all ingredients except tomatoes. Set aside. Cut off ½-inch slice from top of each tomato. Scoop out tomato pulp, leaving a ¼-inch shell. Dice pulp and add to bowl with other ingredients. Stuff each tomato shell with an even portion of mixture. Arrange on glass baking dish in a circle. Cover; cook on **HIGH** for 4 minutes, or until shells are tender, but still firm; turn dish once during cooking.

My cooking time: ______

Tomato Casserole

TOTAL COOKING TIME: 6 minutes
Serves 4
1-quart covered glass casserole dish

2 tablespoons butter
4 medium tomatoes, quartered
1 small onion, diced
1 teaspoon salt
Dash pepper
1 cup seasoned croutons
2 tablespoons grated Parmesan cheese
1 tablespoon chopped parsley

In glass casserole, cook butter on **HIGH** for 1 minute, or until melted. Add tomatoes, onion, salt and pepper. Cover; cook on **HIGH** for 5 minutes; stirring once during cooking. Toss in croutons. Sprinkle with parsley and Parmesan cheese.

My cooking time: ______

Scalloped Potatoes

TOTAL COOKING TIME: 26 minutes
Serves 4 to 6
3-quart covered glass casserole dish

3 tablespoons butter
3 tablespoons flour
1 teaspoon salt
½ teaspoon pepper
3 cups milk
½ cup diced onion
4 medium thin skinned potatoes, peeled

In glass casserole, combine all ingredients except potatoes. Cover; cook on **HIGH** for 10 to 12 minutes, or until thickened; stir twice during cooking. Cut potatoes in half lengthwise, then into ¼-inch slices. Add to thickened sauce. Cover; cook on **HIGH** for 17 to 20 minutes or until potatoes are tender; stir once during cooking.

My cooking time: ______

◄ *Corn Stuffed Tomatoes*

Pepper

Potatoes Savory

TOTAL COOKING TIME: 7 minutes
Serves 4
1-quart covered glass casserole dish

- 1 cup milk
- ¾ cup water
- 2 tablespoons butter
- ½ teaspoon salt
- 1½ cups potato flakes
- ½ cup sour cream
- ½ teaspoon onion powder
- 1 egg, lightly beaten
- ¼ cup grated Cheddar cheese

In glass casserole dish, combine milk, water, butter and salt. Cover; cook on **HIGH** for 5 to 6 minutes, or until mixture boils. Add potato flakes, sour cream, onion powder, egg and cheese. Mix thoroughly. Cover; cook on HIGH for 1 minute or until cheese is melted.

My cooking time: ☐

Peas with Onions and Mushrooms

TOTAL COOKING TIME: 13 minutes
Serves 4
1-quart covered glass casserole dish

- 2 tablespoons butter
- 1 small onion, diced
- ¼ pound mushrooms, sliced
- 2 packages (10-ounces each) frozen peas
- ¼ teaspoon salt
- Dash pepper

In glass casserole, cook butter on **HIGH** for 1 minute, or until melted. Add diced onion and sliced mushrooms. Cook on **HIGH** for 3 minutes or until onions are transparent. Add frozen peas. Cover; cook on **HIGH** for 7 to 9 minutes or until peas are hot, stirring once during cooking. Add salt and pepper.

My cooking time: ☐

Gingery Orange Carrots

TOTAL COOKING TIME: 9 minutes
Serves 4
1-quart covered glass casserole

- 3 tablespoons butter
- 1 tablespoon brown sugar
- ½ teaspoon salt
- ¼ teaspoon ground ginger
- 1 pound carrots, peeled and cut into 2-inch chunks
- 2 small oranges, peeled and sectioned

In glass casserole, cook butter on **HIGH** for 1¼ minutes or until melted. Mix in brown sugar, ginger and salt. Add carrots and orange sections, mixing until coated. Cover; cook on **HIGH** for 7 minutes or until carrots are tender; stir once during cooking.

My cooking time: ☐

Cheesy Cauliflower

TOTAL COOKING TIME: 12 minutes
Serves 4
1-quart glass casserole dish
2-cup glass measuring cup

- 1 pound cauliflower, cut into flowerets
- 2 tablespoon butter
- 2 tablespoon flour
- 1 cup milk
- ½ cup grated Swiss cheese
- 1 teaspoon Worcestershire sauce

Place cauliflower in glass casserole. Cover; cook on **HIGH** for 7 minutes or until tender. Set aside. To make sauce: In glass measure, cook butter on **HIGH** for 1¼ minutes, or until melted. Stir in flour, milk, cheese and Worcestershire sauce. Cook on **HIGH** for 4 minutes or until thick, stirring once during cooking. Pour sauce over cooked cauliflower. Serve hot.

My cooking time: ☐

◄ *Peas with Onions and Mushroomes.*

Brussels Sprouts Sauté

TOTAL COOKING TIME: 9 minutes
Serves 4
1-quart covered glass casserole dish

3 tablespoons butter
1 pound fresh brussels sprouts
½ teaspoon salt
½ teaspoon caraway seeds

In glass casserole, cook butter on **HIGH** for 1½ minutes or until melted. Mix in brussel sprouts, caraway seeds and salt. Cover; cook on **HIGH** for 7 minutes or until tender.

My cooking time: ☐

Broccoli au Gratin

TOTAL COOKING TIME: 13 minutes
Serves 4
1-quart covered glass casserole dish

1 package (10 ounces) frozen broccoli spears
2 tablespoons flour
1 cup milk
½ cup shredded Swiss or Cheddar cheese
Salt and pepper to taste
¼ cup bread crumbs

In original package with outer wrapper removed, cook broccoli on **HIGH** for 3 minutes. Open package, separate stalks to allow remaining ice crystals to dissolve and cook on **HIGH** for 3 minutes longer. Set aside. In glass casserole, cook butter on **HIGH** for 1¼ minutes, or until melted. Stir in flour, then milk. Cover; cook on **HIGH** for 3 to 4 minutes or until thick, stirring once during cooking. Add broccoli, sprinkle wih bread crumbs and cook on **HIGH** for 1½ minutes longer.

My cooking time: ☐

Harvard Beets

TOTAL COOKING TIME: 8 minutes
Serves 4
1-quart covered glass casserole dish

⅓ cup white distilled vineger
¼ cup sugar
1 tablespoon cornstarch
1 can (16 ounces) sliced beets; drain and reserve 1 cup liquid

In glass casserole dish, combine all ingredients except drained beets. Cook on **HIGH** for 5 minutes or until mixture thickens; stir once during cooking. Add beets. Cover; cook on **HIGH** for 3 minutes or until beets are hot.

My cooking time: ☐

TIP: If there is less than 1 cup beet liquid, add enough water to equal 1 cup.

Holiday Yams

TOTAL COOKING TIME: 15 minutes
Serves 4 to 6
2-quart glass serving dish

4 large yams, peeled and sliced
⅔ cup packed brown sugar
¼ cup butter
1 tablespoon brandy
Dash cinnamon
1 large orange, sliced

Arrange yams in glass serving dish. Cover; cook on **HIGH** for 15 minutes or until tender; stir twice during cooking. Remove yams from oven and mash.Add brown sugar, butter, brandy and cinnamon. Mix well. Garnish with sliced oranges.

My cooking time: ☐

◄ *Holiday Yams*

Cheesy Onion Bake

TOTAL COOKING TIME: 12 minutes
Serves 4
1-quart glass serving bowl

2 cups milk
3 tablespoons flour
3 tablespoons butter
1 cup Cheddar cheese, grated
2 cans (16-ounces each) onions, drained
1 can (3-ounces) French fried onion rings

In glass serving bowl, combine milk, flour, butter and Cheddar cheese. Cook on **HIGH** for 8 to 9 minutes or until thickened, stirring twice during cooking. Add canned onions and French fried onion rings. Cook on **HIGH** for 3 minutes or until onions are hot.

My cooking time: ☐

Asparagus Amandine

TOTAL COOKING TIME: 8 minutes
Serves 4
10 x 6 x 1½-inch glass baking dish

3 tablespoons butter
1 cup (3-ounces) sliced almonds
1 tablespoon soy sauce
1 pound fresh asparagus spears, washed

In glass baking dish, cook butter on **HIGH** for 1 minute or until melted. Add remaining ingredients. Cover; cook on **HIGH** for 7 minutes or until asparagus are tender.

My cooking time: ☐

Banquet Peas

TOTAL COOKING TIME: 10 minutes
Serves 4 to 6
1-quart glass casserole dish

2 packages (10-ounces each) frozen peas in cream sauce
1 can (3-ounces) French-fried onion rings
½ cup sliced almonds
½ cup grated Cheddar cheese
2 tablespoons dried chopped parsley flakes.

In glass casserole, combine all ingredients. Cover; cook on **HIGH** for 8 to 10 minutes or until mixture is hot and cheese is melted; stir once during cooking.

My cooking time: ☐

Glazed Carrots

TOTAL COOKING TIME: 9 minutes
Serves 4
1-quart covered glass casserole dish

4 tablespoons butter
2 tablespoons brown sugar
1 pound carrots, peeled and cut into 1-inch chunks

In glass casserole, cook butter on **HIGH** for 1¼ minutes or until melted. Mix in brown sugar. Add carrots and stir until evenly coated. Cover; cook on **HIGH** for 7 minutes, or until carrots are tender.

My cooking time: ☐

Spinach Supreme

TOTAL COOKING TIME: 5 minutes
Serves 4
1-quart glass serving dish

1 package (10-ounces) frozen chopped spinach
½ cup sour cream
2 tablespoons dry onion soup mix
2 tablespoons lemon juice

In original package, with outer wrapper removed, cook frozen spinach on **HIGH** for 4 minutes or until hot. Place into serving dish and mix in remaining ingredients. Cover; cook on **HIGH** for 1 minute, or until mixture is hot.

My cooking time: ☐

Pasta, Rice & Cereal

Carefree Cooking is a good discription of the ease in preparing pasta, rice or hot cereals in the microwave oven. Rice cooks in less time with the same light fluffy testure. Hot cereals turn out smooth every time without the messy pan to wash. Single servings can even be made right in the cereal bowl.

As a General Rule: Pasta and Rice

- Cook covered in **large** glass or ceramic dish. Should be at least 2-quart size.
- Bring water to a boil before adding pasta.
- Rice can be added to hot tap water and cooked in one step.

Microwave Method: Pasta and Rice

Rice and pasta products both cook by absorbing water. This can be done in a microwave oven by using the following method and charts which give amounts and times.

PASTA:
1. Place water in large glass container and cover.
2. Cook on power level **HIGH** until water boils.
3. Add salt, oil and pasta.
4. Set power level and time recommended on Pasta Cooking Chart. Cook as instructed.
5. Drain and serve or combine with other ingredients as desired.

RICE:
1. Place water and rice in large glass container and cover.
2. Set power level and time recommended on Rice Cooking Chart. Cook as instructed.
3. Allow to stand 5 minutes.
4. Fluff with fork and serve.

My Notes:

PASTA COOKING CHART

ITEM	COOKING CONTAINER	HOT WATER	PASTA	ADDING	COOKING PROCEDURE
Lasagna	11x7-inch Glass Baking Dish	6 cups	8 oz.	1 tsp. Salt 1 Tbls. oil	HIGH (9) Heat water 10–12 min. (covered) Add Lasagna. MED (3) : 11–13 min. (covered)
Macaroni	2 qt. Casserole	6 cups	7 oz.	1 tsp. Salt 1 Tbls. Oil	HIGH (9) Heat water 10–12 min. (covered) Add macaroni. MED (3) : 9–11 min. (covered)
Spaghetti	2 qt. Casserole	6 cups	7 oz.	1 tsp. Salt 1 Tbls. Oil	HIGH (9) Heat water 10–12 min. (covered) Add noodles. MED (3) : 12–15 min. (covered)
Rigatoni	2 qt. Casserole	6 cups	12 oz.	1 tsp. Salt 1 Tbls. Oil	HIGH (9) Heat water 12–15 min. (covered) Add rigatoni. MED (3) : 14–16 min. (covered)

RICE COOKING CHART

ITEM	COOKING CONTAINER	HOT WATER	RICE	ADDING	COOKING PROCEDURE
Long Grain Rice	2 qt.	2 cups	1 cup	1 tsp. Salt	HIGH (9) 11–12 min.
Short Grain Rice	2 qt.	2 cups	1 cup	1 tsp. Salt	HIGH (9) 11–12 min.
Wild and White Rice Casserole Mix	2 qt.	2 cups	6 oz. pkg.	1 tsp. Salt	HIGH (9) 15 min.
Quick Cooking RIce	1 qt.	1 cup	1 cup	1 tsp. Salt	HIGH (9) 3–4 min. Standing 5 min.
Brown Rice	2 qt. Covered Glass Bowl	1 cup	1 cup	1 tsp. Salt	HIGH (9) 25 minutes
Cereal Barley	2 qt. Covered Glass Bowl	4 cups	1 cup	1 tsp. Salt	HIGH (9) 25 minutes

As a General Rule: Hot Cereals

- Cook uncovered in large glass measuring cup. It's easy to handle and the cereal can be poured right into the bowl.
- Use a wire whip to stir and lumps will never be a problem.
- Always start with cold water or milk and cereal in cooking utensil.
- Always cook on power level **HIGH**.
- Always stir mixture after the first 2 minutes of cooking time. This is very important. It redistributes the starch throughout the liquid.
- Always let cereal stand a few minutes before serving, if recommended on cereal package.

Microwave Method: Hot Cereals

Cereal like pasta and rice, also cook by absorption of water, so, it is best to follow directions on cereal package as to how long to cook the cereal. Example: If directions call for boiling it for 2 minutes, then bring it to a boil in the microwave oven and allow it to boil for 2 minutes. Below is the most successful method for cooking hot cereals:

1. Place desired amount of **COLD** water or milk in large glass measuring cup or bowl.
2. Add desired amount of cereal.
3. Stir with wire whip or fork.
4. Heat in microwave oven for 2 minutes on power level **HIGH**.
5. **Important** — Stir to redistribute any cereal which is at the bottom of the bowl.
6. Continue to cook at the same power level until the cereal boils and is desired thickness, according to package instructions. Approximate times are given on the Hot Cereal Cooking Chart.
7. Some cereals should stand a few minutes before serving. Follow the directions on package.

HOT CEREAL COOKING CHART

Amount	Cooking Time at Power Level HIGH
1 Serving	3 min.
2 Servings	4 min.
4 Servings	6 min.

Popeye Rice

TOTAL COOKING TIME: 17 minutes
Serves 4 to 6
2-quart glass bowl

2 cups water
1 cup long-grain rice
1¼ cups fresh chopped spinach
¼ cup chopped green onion
¼ cup chopped celery
2 tablespoons lemon juice
¼ cup chopped parsley
1½ teaspoons salt

Place all ingredients in glass bowl. Cover; cook on **HIGH** for 15 to 17 minutes or until liquid is almost absorbed; stir 3 times during cooking. Let sit covered, for 5 minutes or until remaining liquid is absorbed.

My cooking time:

South of the Border Rice

TOTAL COOKING TIME: 17 minutes
Serves 4
11 x 7 inch glass baking dish
4-quart glass bowl

6 slices uncooked bacon
¾ cup water
1 can (16-ounces) whole tomatoes, undrained and chopped
1 package (6-ounces) Spanish rice mix
6 stuffed green olives, sliced

In glass baking dish, cook bacon, on **HIGH** for 5 minutes or until cooked. Drain and reserve drippings. In glass bowl, combine bacon drippings, water, tomatoes and Spanish rice mix. Cover; cook on **HIGH** for 12 minutes or until liquid is almost completely absorbed. Crumble bacon and mix into rice. Garnish with sliced olives.

My cooking time:

Cheesy Rice

TOTAL COOKING TIME: 15 minutes
Serves 4
2-quart glass bowl

2 cups water
1 cup long-grain rice
8 ounces grated Cheddar cheese (about 2 cups)
1 teaspoon salt
½ teaspoon garlic powder
2 cups milk
1 tablespoon chopped parsley
¼ cup grated Parmesan cheese
¼ cup slivered almonds
Salt to taste

In glass bowl, combine water, rice, cheese, salt, garlic powder and milk. Cover; cook on **HIGH** for 12 minutes or until most all liquid is absorbed; stir twice during cooking. Stir in remaining ingredients. Let sit, covered, for 5 minutes for remaining liquid to be absorbed.

My cooking time:

Granola

TOTAL COOKING TIME: 11 minutes
1 quart glass bowl
13 x 9 inch glass dish

⅔ cup raisins
¼ cup packed brown sugar
¼ cup salad oil
¼ cup honey
4 cups rolled oats
½ cup sliced almonds
¼ cup wheat germ
Dash each cinnamon, cloves, nutmeg, salt

Soak raisins in hot water to cover for 10 minutes or until plump; drain. In glass bowl, combine sugar, oil and honey; cook on **HIGH** for 1 minute or until sugar is melted, stir well. In larger glass dish, mix together rolled oats, almonds, wheat germ, and spices. Pour sugar mixture over dry ingredients; mix well. Cook on **HIGH** for 10 minutes; stir every two minutes to avoid burning in spots.

My cooking time:

Macabeef

TOTAL COOKING TIME: 16 minutes
Serves 4
2-quart glass casserole dish

1 pound lean ground beef
4 cups cooked macaroni
1 jar (16-ounces) spaghetti sauce
Salt to taste

In glass casserole, cook beef on **HIGH** for 5 minutes or until no longer pink. Drain. Stir in remaining ingredients. Cover; cook on **HIGH** for 10 minutes or until hot.

My cooking time: ____

Cheesy Linguini

TOTAL COOKING TIME: 27 minutes
Serves 4
2-quart glass casserole dish
2-quart glass bowl

6 cups water
8 ounces linguini or spaghetti
1 tablespoon oil
2 tablespoons butter
2 tablespoons flour
2 cups milk
1 cup grated Cheddar cheese
¼ cup grated Parmesan cheese
1 teaspoon garlic powder
1 tablespoon chopped parsley
Salt to taste

Place water and salt in glass casserole. Cover; cook on **HIGH** for 10 minutes or until boiling. Add pasta and oil. Cover; cook on **MED/DEF** for 10 minutes or until tender. Drain and place in serving dish. Cook butter on **HIGH** for 1 minute, or until melted. Stir in flour and milk. Cook on **HIGH** for 4 to 6 minutes or until thick. Stir in cheeses and garlic powder. Pour over pasta, sprinkle with parsley.

My cooking time: ____

Lasagna

TOTAL COOKING TIME: 41 minutes
Serves 4 to 6
11 x 7-inch glass baking dish
1½-quart glass casserole dish

6 cups water
8 ounces lasagna noodles
1 teaspoon salt
1 tablespoon oil
1 pound lean ground beef
½ cup diced onion
1 jar (32-ounces) spaghetti sauce
1 jar (4-ounces) sliced mushrooms, drained
2 cups cottage cheese
1 egg, lightly beaten
8 ounces Mazzarella cheese, sliced

Place water and salt in glass baking dish. Cover; cook on **HIGH** for 10 to 12 minutes, or until boiling. Add lasagna noodles and oil. Cover; cook on **MED/DEF** for 11 to 13 minutes or until tender. Drain water and separate noodles to avoid sticking together. In glass casserole cook beef and onion on **HIGH** for 5 minutes or until beef is no longer pink. Drain Mix in spaghetti sauce and mushrooms. Mix together egg and cottage cheese. In glass baking dish, layer ⅓ of noodles, ⅓ sauce and then ½ cottage cheese-egg mixture. Repeat layers two more times, omitting cottage cheese from third layer. Cover; cook on **HIGH** for 10 minutes; arrange Mozzarella cheese on top during last 5 minutes of cooking.

My cooking time: ____

◄ *Macabeef*

Mock Manicotti

TOTAL COOKING TIME: 29 minutes
Serves 4
2-quart glass casserole dish

6 cups water
1 teaspoon salt
1 tablespoon oil
8 ounces wide egg noodles
1 pound lean ground beef
1 jar (15 to 16-ounces) spaghetti sauce
2 cups cottage cheese
1 egg, slightly beaten
1 tablespoon chopped parsley
1 scallion, chopped

Place water and salt in glass casserole. Cover; cook on **HIGH** for 10 minutes or until boiling. Add noodles and oil, cover, cook on **MED/DEF** for 8 to 10 minutes, or until noodles are tender. In small glass casserole, cook beef on **HIGH** for 5 minutes or until no longer pink. Drain. Add spaghetti sauce. Combine cottage cheese, egg, scallion and parsley. Layer half of noodles in casserole, then cottage cheese mixture, remaining noodles and beef mixture. Cover; cook on **HIGH** for 10 minutes or until hot.

My cooking time: ____

Macaroni and Cheese

TOTAL COOKING TIME: 29 minutes
Serves 4
3-quart covered glass casserole dish
2-cup glass bowl

6 cups water
1 teaspoon salt
2½ cups uncooked macaroni
1 tablespoon oil
2 tablespoons butter
2 tablespoons flour
½ cup milk
2 cups grated Cheddar cheese
½ teaspoon prepared mustard
¼ teaspoon salt
¼ cup bread crumbs

Place water and salt in glass casserole. Cover; cook on **HIGH** for 10 to 12 minutes or until boiling. Add macaroni and oil. Cook on **MED/DEF** for 8 to 10 minutes or until soft. Drain. Set aside. In glass bowl, cook butter on **HIGH** for 1 minute or until melted. Stir in flour, then milk. Cook on **HIGH** for 4 minutes or until thick; stir once during cooking. Stir in cheese and seasonings, mixing briskly until cheese melts. Mix into cooked macaroni. Add bread crumbs and stir well. Cover; cook on **HIGH** for 5 minutes or until hot.

My cooking time: ____

Orange Rice

TOTAL COOKING TIME: 16 minutes
Serves 4
2-quart glass bowl

¼ cup butter
1 cup finely diced celery
¼ cup finely diced onion
1½ cups orange juice
½ cup water
1 teaspoon salt
1½ cups long-grain rice
1 tablespoon chopped parsley
1 orange, sliced
½ cup sliced toasted almonds

In large glass bowl, cook butter on **HIGH** for 1¼ minutes or until melted. Add celery and onion. Cook on **HIGH** for 2 minutes or until vegetables are cooked. Mix in orange juice, water, and salt. Cover; cook on **HIGH** for 6 minutes or until boiling. Add rice, cover, cook on **MED/DEF** for 12 minutes or until liquid is almost absorbed. Let sit covered, for 5 minutes or until liquid is absorbed. Garnish with orange slices and almonds.

My cooking time: ____

◄ *Orange Rice*

Noodle Ring

TOTAL COOKING TIME: 16 minutes
Serves 4 to 6
1½-quart round glass baking dish
or tube microwave dish

4 ounces medium egg noodles
1 cup toasted bread crumbs
2 tablespoons butter
2 eggs
¾ cup cottage cheese
1 cup sour cream
3 tablespoons minced green onion
2 tablespoons minced green pepper
2 tablespoons minced pimiento
1 tablespoon minced parsley
½ teaspoon Worcestershire sauce
1 teaspoon salt
Dash pepper
Dash garlic salt

Cook noodles according to directions; drain. In glass baking dish cook butter on **HIGH** for 1 minute to melt. Stir in bread crumbs. Press crumbs firmly onto bottom and sides of dish. Place small drinking glass in center of glass baking dish to create ring shape. Beat eggs in large bowl, blend in remaining ingredients.
Fold noodles into sauce and pour into mold. Cook on **MED/DEF** for 12 to 15 minutes, rotating dish twice. Allow to stand 5 minutes before unmolding. Loosen edge with knife and invert onto serving platter. If desired garnish with parsley and fill center with peas or creamed meat.

My cooking time:

Curried Rice

TOTAL COOKING TIME: 4 minutes
Serves 6
1-quart glass casserole dish

¼ cup chopped onion
¼ cup chopped green pepper
2 tablespoons butter
3 cups hot cooked rice
½ teaspoon curry powder
¾ teaspoon salt

In glass casserole combine onion, green pepper, and butter. Cook on **HIGH** for 2 minutes, or until onion is soft. Add remaining ingredients, mixing well. Cover; cook on **HIGH** for 2 minutes to heat through.

My cooking time:

Confetti Rice

TOTAL COOKING TIME: 21 minutes
Serves 6
2-quart glass casserole dish

½ cup chopped onions
½ cup sliced mushrooms
3 tablespoons butter
2 cups hot water
2 cubes chicken bouillon
1 cup long grain rice
1 package (10-ounces) frozen peas and carrots, defrosted
½ teaspoon salt
Pepper to taste

In glass casserole combine onion, mushrooms and butter. Cook on **HIGH** for 3 minutes, or until onions are soft. Add water, bouillon cubes and rice. Cover; cook on **HIGH** for 10 minutes. Stir in peas and carrots. Cover; cook on **HIGH** for 6 to 8 minutes. Add salt and pepper before serving.

My cooking time:

Almond Sesame Noodles

TOTAL COOKING TIME: 12 minutes
Serves 6
2-quart glass casserole dish

8 ounces medium egg noodles
¼ cup butter
½ cup toasted almonds
2 tablespoons toasted sesame seeds

Cook noodles as directed, until tender. Place butter in glass casserole. Cook on **HIGH** for 1 minute to melt. Stir in seeds and nuts. Add noodles, tossing to coat.

My cooking time:

TIPS: To toast almonds, spread in glass pie plate. Cook on **HIGH** for 6 to 7 minutes, until golden. Stir frequently. To toast sesame seeds, spread on glass pie plate. Cook on **HIGH** for 3 to 4 minutes until golden. Stir frequently.

Yeast & Quick Breads

Use your microwave oven as a time saver when making breads. Both the fermenting and proofing steps can be done in one hour rather than the four hours it takes conventionally. Quick breads require less cooking time when done in the microwave oven. Try the package mixes or scratch recipes in a ring shape for an unusual shaped party loaf.

As a General Rule: Yeast Breads

- Yeast bread dough will ferment (first rising) and proof (second rising) very quickly in the microwave oven.
- Although bread can be baked in the microwave oven, the crust will not brown and the texture will not be as fine as when cooked conventionally.
- Always use glass bowl for fermenting bread and glass loaf pan for proofing bread in microwave oven.

Microwave Method: Yeast Breads

No yeast bread recipes have been given in this chapter. Prepare your favorite dough and use the steps below for fermenting and proofing.

FERMENTING AND PROOFING FRESH DOUGH:

1. While kneading the dough, heat 2 cups water in the microwave oven on power level **HIGH**, for 5 minutes.
2. Place dough in greased glass bowl, turn over and cover with a cloth.
3. Place dough in microwave oven with water and cook for 15 minutes on power level **MED/DEF**. Bread should be doubled in volume.
4. Fold dough over several times, shape into loaf or rolls and repeat step 3 for proofing.

PROOFING FROZEN DOUGH:

1. Heat water as directed above and place frozen dough in glass loaf pan in microwave oven.
2. Cook for 30 seconds on power level **HIGH**. Let dough set for 20 minutes.
3. Repeat as necessary.

BAKING YEAST BREADS:

NOTE: We recommend breads be baked conventionally, but have included microwave instructions for your reference.

1. Cook uncovered, one loaf at a time.
2. Cook on power level **HIGH** for 7 minutes or until bread sounds hollow when tapped.
3. If brown crust is desired place bread in hot (500°F) conventional oven for 8–10 minutes.

As a General Rule: Quick Breads

- Cook covered with wax paper for first half of cooking time.
- Cook in glass loaf pan for breads, for muffins use muffin liners in custard cups or special microwave cupcake pan.
- Test for doneness with a toothpick as you would conventionally.
- Fill loaf pan no more than half full and run knife lengthwise through batter before cooking.

Microwave Method: Quick Breads

Prepare your favorite batter using the general rules just given and cook according to the steps below.

1. Pour batter into a glass loaf pan.
2. Begin cooking for time recommended on Quick Bread Cooking Chart, on power level MED/DEF.
3. Finish cooking on power level HIGH for remaining time given on Quick Bread Cooking Chart.

QUICK BREAD COOKING CHART

Amount	Time at Power Level MED/DEF	HIGH
1 ring shape	6 min.	3 min.
1 loaf 8″ x 4″	7 min.	2–3 min.
6 Muffins	4–5 min.	

TIP: When cooking muffins proper arrangement in the oven will assist in even cooking. Use the proper arrangement guide in the first section of this book. A microwave cupcake pan places the muffins in the proper arrangement.

My Notes:

Old Fashion Pumpkin Bread

TOTAL COOKING TIME: 14 minutes
Makes 1 loaf or ring
Tube microwave dish or glass loaf dish

1¼ cups flour
1½ cups sugar
1 teaspoon baking soda
¾ teaspoon cinnamon
½ teaspoon cloves
½ teaspoon nutmeg
1 cup canned pumpkin
2 eggs
1 teaspoon vanilla
¾ cup chopped walnuts
½ cup oil
⅓ cup water

Mix together dry ingredients, then in separate bowl, mix together remaining ingredients. Combine and mix just until moist. Pour into glass baking dish. Cook on **MED/DEF** for 9 minutes, then on **HIGH** for 5 minutes.

My cooking time: ☐

Sticky Biscuit Ring

TOTAL COOKING TIME: 11 minutes
Makes 1 ring
Tube microwave dish

1 package (10-ounces) flaky refrigerated biscuits
1½ cups brown sugar
½ cup butter
½ teaspoon grated orange peel
½ teaspoon cinnamon
½ cup chopped nuts

In glass bowl, cook sugar and butter on **HIGH** for 1¼ minutes, or until melted; stir well. Mix in nuts, orange peel and cinnamon. Separate each biscuit into 3 layers. Spread just enough sweet mixture on bottom of tube microwave dish to coat. Top with half of biscuit pieces. Repeat with remaining biscuit pieces and sweet mixture. Cook on **HIGH** for 5 minutes or until done. Do not overcook or biscuits will become hard.

My cooking time: ☐

◄ *Old Fashion Pumpkin Bread.*

Boston Brown Bread

TOTAL COOKING TIME: 7 minutes
1-quart glass measuring cup, greased
glass serving platter

1 cup whole wheat flour
½ cup corn meal
½ cup 100% bran breakfast cereal
¼ cup raisins
¼ cup chopped walnuts
1 teaspoon baking soda
½ teaspoon salt
1 cup buttermilk
⅓ cup molasses

In mixing bowl thoroughly combine all dry ingredients, then add liquid ingredients. Stir just until combined. Pour ingredients into greased glass measuring cup. Cover tightly with plastic wrap. Cook on **HIGH** for 5 minutes. Let sit for 5 minutes. Turn out onto glass serving platter. Cook on **HIGH** for 2 minutes to insure doneness.

My cooking time: ☐

Garlic Bread

TOTAL COOKING TIME: 5 minutes
Makes 1 loaf
Wax paper

1 large loaf French bread
6 tablespoons butter
1 tablespoon Parmesan cheese
1 teaspoon garlic powder
1 teaspoon Italian seasoning
½ teaspoon paprika

Slice bread but do not cut all the way through loaf. Cook butter on **MED/DEF** for 1½ minutes or until soft, but not melted. Add seasonings; mix well. Spread butter mixture evenly between slices. Loosely wrap wax paper around bread; cook on **HIGH** for 2 minutes or until hot.

My cooking time: ______

Sauce Sweet & Savory

Whether you're making a favorite chocolate sauce, cherries jubilee or gravy for Thanksgiving dinner, you'll love the ease of preparing these in the microwave oven. Arm yourself with a large glass measuring cup and a wire whip so that smooth, flavorful sauces and gravies are yours every time.

As a General Rule

- Use a glass bowl or large glass measuring cup.
- Cook on power level **HIGH** for all sauces.
- Cook uncovered.
- Stir at least once during cooking time.
- Use a wire whip for stirring sauces as they thicken in order to avoid lumps.

Microwave Method:

Regardless if you are making a dessert sauce or gravy the method is the same. Charts on the next few pages give cooking times for white sauces or gravies.

CORNSTARCH THICKENED SAUCES:

1. Combine cornstarch and liquid in large glass measuring cup.
2. Stir with wire whip and cook on power level **HIGH** until boiling and thickened approximately 3 minutes per cup of liquid.
3. **Stir once after first 2 minutes of cooking time.**
4. Add fruit and other ingredients and cook until heated throughout approximately 2 minutes.

FLOUR THICKENED SAUCES:

1. Combine flour and fat in large glass measuring cup.
2. Cook until fat is melted. Stir to mix flour and fat.
3. Add liquid. Stir with wire whip until smooth.
4. Cook on power level **HIGH** for 2 minutes
5. **Stir well to redistribute flour throughout liquid**
6. Continue cooking on same power level until mixture boils and thickens approximately 4 minutes per cup.
7. Cook an additional 3 minutes to reduce the flour taste.
8. Add any other ingredients at this time and heat additionally as necessary.

White Sauce

TOTAL COOKING TIME: 8 minutes
Makes 2 cups
4-cup glass measure

In glass measure cook butter on **HIGH** for time recommended on chart. With wire whip, blend in flour, then milk. Cook on **HIGH** for time recommended on chart; stir once during cooking. Add salt to taste.

	THIN	MEDIUM	THICK
Butter	2 tablespoons	4 tablespoons	6 tablespoons
Flour	2 tablespoons	4 tablespoons	6 tablespoons
Milk	2 cups	2 cups	2 cups
Salt	to taste	to taste	to taste
Power Level	HIGH	HIGH	HIGH
Cooking Time/Butter	1 min.	1¼ min.	1½ min.
Cooking Time/Sauce	8 min.	8 min.	8 min.

Brown Gravy

TOTAL COOKING TIME: 8 minutes
Makes 2-cups
4-cup glass measure

In glass measure combine fat and flour with wire whip. Stir in liquid. Cook on **HIGH** for time recommended on chart. Stir once during cooking time.

	THIN	MEDIUM	THICK
Fat	2 tablespoons	4 tablespoons	6 tablespoons
Flour	2 tablespoons	4 tablespoons	6 tablespoons
Liquid (Drippings + Water)	2 cups	2 cups	2 cups
Salt	to taste	to taste	to taste
Power Level	HIGH	HIGH	HIGH
Cooking Time	8 min.	8 min.	8 min.

Custard Sauce

TOTAL COOKING TIME: 6 minutes
Makes 2 cups
1-quart glass measuring cup

2 cups milk
3 eggs
¾ cup sugar
⅛ teaspoon salt
1 teaspoon vanilla

In glass measure combine milk, eggs, sugar and salt. Beat well with wire whip. Cook on **HIGH** for 6 minutes or until thick; stir once during cooking.

My cooking time: ______

Sauce Sweet & Savory

Apple-Prune Topping

TOTAL COOKING TIME: 5 minutes
Makes 1 cup
1-pint glass bowl

2 tablespoons brown sugar
1 tablespoon cornstarch
1 cup apple juice
½ cup diced apples
¼ cup chopped pitted prunes
1 teaspoon lemon juice
Dash each salt and allspice

In glass bowl, mix together brown sugar and cornstarch. Blend in apple juice and cook on **HIGH** for 2½ minutes or until thick; stir once during cooking. Mix in apples and prunes. Cook on **HIGH** for 2 minutes. Sprinkle with lemon juice and season to taste with salt and allspice.

My cooking time: ______

Apple Country Ham Sauce

TOTAL COOKING TIME: 5 minutes
Makes 2 cups
1-quart glass bowl

½ cup ham drippings
½ cup diced onion
½ cup corn syrup
½ cup raisins
3 tablespoons molasses
2 tablespoons cornstarch
1 tablespoon lemon juice
½ teaspoon salt
¼ teaspoon cinnamon
1½ cups grated apple (about 3 large apples)

In glass bowl, cook ham drippings and onion on **HIGH** for 2 minutes or until onion is tender. Stir in remaining ingredients except grated apples; cook on **HIGH** for 3 minutes or until thickened. Stir in grated apples. Serve over ham steaks.

My cooking time: ______

Bittersweet Chocolate Fondue

TOTAL COOKING TIME: 3½ minutes
Makes 2½ cups
4-quart glass serving bowl

1 package (12-ounces) semi-sweet chocolate pieces (2 cups)
2 squares (1-ounce each) baking chocolate
1½ cup light cream
1 teaspoon vanilla extract

In glass serving bowl, combine chocolates and cook on **HIGH** for 3 minutes or until melted, stirring once during cooking. With wire whip, stir in cream and vanilla. Cook on **HIGH** for 20 seconds, or until mixture is smooth.

My cooking time: ______

TIP: An excellent fondue for fresh or frozen fruit chunks.

Butterscotch Topping

TOTAL COOKING TIME: 8 minutes
Makes 1¾ cups
2-quart glass serving bowl

½ cup butter
1 cup packed brown sugar
¼ cup milk

In glass serving bowl cook butter on **MED/DEF** for 1¾ minutes, or until melted. Stir in sugar and milk. Cover; cook on **HIGH** for 6 minutes, or until syrupy; stir once during cooking. Serve warm.

My cooking time: ______

◄ *Apple Country Ham Sauce*

Speedy Hollandaise Sauce

TOTAL COOKING TIME: 3 minutes
Makes ¾ cup
2-cup glass measuring cup

½ cup butter
1 egg, slightly beaten
2 tablespoon lemon juice

In glass measuring cup cook butter on **HIGH** for 1¼ minutes, or until melted. With wire whip, beat in egg. Cook on **MED/DEF** for 1 minute. Egg will appear slightly set. Stir in lemon juice and quickly beat with wire whip to prevent lumping.

My cooking time:

Bechamél Sauce

TOTAL COOKING TIME: 4½ minutes
Makes 1 cup
2-cup glass measuring cup

2 tablespoons butter
1 tablespoon diced onion
1 tablespoon flour
1 cup light cream
1 cube chicken boullion

In glass measuring cup cook butter on **MED/DEF** for 45 seconds or until melted. Add onion and cook on **HIGH** for 1 minute or until onion is transparent. Stir in remaining ingredients. Cook on **HIGH** for 3 to 3½ minutes or until sauce is thickened. Stir once during cooking.

My cooking time:

Barbecue Sauce

TOTAL COOKING TIME: 7 minutes
Makes 1½ cups
2-cup glass measuring cup

1 tablespoon butter
1 tablespoon diced green pepper
1 tablespoon diced onion
1 can (8-ounces) tomato sauce
¼ cup wine vinegar
2 tablespoons brown sugar
1 tablespoon Worcestershire sauce

In glass measuring cup cook butter on **MED/DEF** for 30 seconds, or until melted. Add green pepper and onion. Cook on **HIGH** for 2 minutes, or until onion is transparent. Stir in remaining ingredients. Cover; cook on **HIGH** for 5 minutes, or until bubbling; stir once during cooking.

My cooking time:

TIP: For thicker sauce, stir in 1 tablespoon flour and return to oven on **HIGH** for 1 minute.

Spaghetti Sauce

TOTAL COOKING TIME: 20 minutes
Makes about 2 quarts
2-quart glass mixing bowl

½ pound lean ground beef
½ cup diced onion
½ cup diced green pepper
1 clove garlic, minced
2 cans (15-ounces each) tomato sauce
1 can (12-ounces) tomato paste
¼ cup wine vinegar
2 tablespoons brown sugar
1 tablespoon Italian spice
2 teaspoons salt

In glass mixing bowl, crumble ground beef and add onion, green pepper, and garlic. Cook on **HIGH** for 5 minutes or until beef is no longer pink; drain. Stir in remaining ingredients. Cover; cook on **HIGH** for 10 minutes, or until bubbling; stir once during cooking. For flavors to combine, cook on **MED/DEF** for 5 minutes.

My cooking time:

Puddings & Custards

Puddings and custards require either a double boiler or constant stirring when prepared conventionally. Not so with microwave cooking. The microwaves don't heat the dish, so there is no out-side heat to scorch or burn the pudding. Once you have made a pudding this way you'll never switch back to the conventional method.

As a General Rule:

- Cook uncovered.
- Cook in large glass measuring cup for ease in pouring to individual servings or pie shell.
- Cook puddings on power level **HIGH**.
- Cook custards on power level **MED/DEF**.

Microwave Method:

Puddings and custards contain sugar as a main ingredient. As a result, they cook fairly quickly, and easily if pepared in the manner described below.

1. Measure liquid in level glass measuring cup. Add package mix, stir to blend with wire whip or fork.
2. Cook for 2 minutes on power level recommended on Pudding and Custard Chart.
3. With a whip or fork, stir to redistribute any starch mixture which may have settled to the bottom. **Very Important Step.**
4. Continue to cook as recommended on chart until pudding thickens or boils as recipe directs.
5. Stir once during second half of cooking.

PACKAGE PUDDING AND CUSTARD COOKING CHART

Amount	PUDDINGS Time at Power Level HIGH (9)	CUSTARDS Time at Power Level MEDIUM (5)	Comments
2 cups	6 – 7 min.	10 – 11 min.	Stir twice during cooking
4 cups	8 – 9 min.	11 – 13 min.	

Rice Pudding

TOTAL COOKING TIME: 14 minutes
Serves 4 to 6
2-quart glass mixing bowl

2 cups milk
2 eggs, slightly beaten
½ cup sugar
½ cup quick cooking rice
½ cup raisins
1 teaspoon grated lemon peel

In glass measuring cup, cook milk on **HIGH** for 3 to 4 minutes to scald. In large glass bowl, combine eggs, sugar, rice, raisins, and lemon peel. Gradually stir heated milk into egg mixture stirring constantly. Cook on **MED/DEF** for 8 to 10 minutes, stirring every 2 minutes until pudding thickens. Serve warm or cool; garnish with whipped cream if desired.

My cooking time: ☐

Lemon Souffle

TOTAL COOKING TIME: 6 minutes
Serves 6 to 8
2-quart glass mixing bowl

½ cup sugar
1 envelope (1 tablespoon) unflavored gelatin
¼ teaspoon salt
1 cup water
3 eggs, separated
¼ cup lemon juice
1 tablespoon grated lemon peel
⅓ cup sugar
1 cup heavy cream, whipped

Prepare 4-cup souffle dish by forming a collar of wax paper around top of dish; set aside. In large glass mixing bowl combine sugar, gelatin, salt, and water, mixing well. Beat in egg yolks until well blended. Cook on **MED/DEF**for 4 to 6 minutes or just until mixture begins to boil, stirring twice with wire whip. Stir in lemon juice and peel. Refrigerate until mixture thickens. Beat egg whites, gradually add sugar, beating until stiff. Fold egg whites and whipped cream into lemon mixture. Spoon into prepared dish. Chill 5 hours. Remove wax paper collar from dish before serving.

My cooking time: ☐

Raspberry Snow

TOTAL COOKING TIME: 5 minutes
Serves 8 to 10
2-quart glass mixing bowl
1½-quart mold

⅔ cup sugar
1 envelope (1 tablespoon) unflavored gelatin
½ teaspoon salt
1¼ cups milk
2 eggs, slightly beaten
2 teaspoons orange liqueur
1⅓ cups (3½-ounce can) flaked coconut
2 cups heavy cream, whipped
Raspberry Sauce

In large glass bowl, mix sugar, gelatin and salt. Add milk and eggs; beat until well blended. Cook on **MED/DEF** for 3 to 5 minutes or until mixture bubbles slightly. Chill until partially set. Add orange liqueur. Fold in coconut, then whipped cream. Pile into 1½-quart mold; chill until firm, at least 4 hours. Unmold. Serve with Raspberry Sauce.

RASPBERRY SAUCE
1 package (10-ounces) frozen raspberries, thawed
½ cup currant jelly
1½ teaspoons cornstarch

In small glass bowl combine raspberries, jelly and cornstarch. Cook on **HIGH** for 5 to 6 minutes until clear and slightly thick. Cool and serve.

My cooking time: ☐

Quick Bread Pudding

TOTAL COOKING TIME: 16 minutes
Serves 6
8-inch round glass dish
1-quart glass measuring cup

3 cups dry bread cubes
2 cups milk
2 eggs
⅓ cup sugar
1 teaspoon vanilla
⅛ teaspoon salt
Dash cinnamon and nutmeg

Place bread cubes in glass dish. Combine remaining ingredients in glass measuring cup. Cook on **HIGH** for 4 to 6 minutes, stirring frequently until mixture begins to thicken slightly. Pour over bread cubes. Sprinkle with cinnamon and nutmeg. Cook on **MED/DEF** for 8 to 10 minutes, rotating dish twice.

My cooking time:

TIP: If desired add ½ cup raisins to milk and egg mixture

Fruit Cream Pudding

TOTAL COOKING TIME: 8 minutes
Serves 6
2-quart glass mixing bowl

½ cup sugar
¼ cup cornstarch
¼ teaspoon salt
2 cups milk
3 eggs separated
1 can (16-ounces) fruit cocktail, well-drained
1 teaspoon vanilla

In large glass bowl, blend sugar, cornstarch and salt. Gradually stir in milk, mixing well. Cook on **HIGH** for 5 to 6 minutes or until thickened; stir twice during cooking. Stir a small amount of hot mixture into egg yolks. Add warmed egg yolks to hot mixture, stirring well with wire whip. Cook on **HIGH** for 1½ to 2 minutes until pudding coats metal spoon. Fold in fruit cocktail and vanilla. Cool slightly. In a separate glass bowl, beat egg whites until stiff peaks form; fold into custard. Chill to serve.

My cooking time:

Surprise Pudding Cake

TOTAL COOKING TIME: 9 minutes
Serves 6
8-inch round glass baking dish

1 cup flour
¾ cup sugar
2 tablespoons plus ¼ cup cocoa
2 teaspoons baking powder
½ teaspoon salt
½ cup chopped nuts
½ cup milk
2 tablespoon oil
1 teaspoon vanilla
¾ cup brown sugar
1½ cups boiling water

Combine flour, sugar, 2 tablespoons cocoa, baking powder, salt, and nuts. Stir in milk, oil and vanilla. Spread batter in glass baking dish. Combine brown sugar and ¼ cup cocoa; sprinkle over top of batter. Pour boiling water over all. Cook on **HIGH** for 8 to 9 minutes until top is set and begins to appear dry. Serve warm or cold. Top with whipped cream if desired.

My cooking time:

Cherry Pie Pudding

TOTAL COOKING TIME: 12 to 15 minutes
Serves 6
1½-quart glass baking dish

1 can (21-ounces) cherry pie filling
1 sponge or angel food cake, cut in cubes
1 cup milk
2 eggs
1 tablespoon sugar
½ teaspoon almond extract
1 can (16-ounces) cherries, pitted and drained

Spread cherry pie filling in glass baking dish. Place cubes of cake on top. Beat together eggs, milk, sugar, and almond extract; pour over cake cubes. Cook on **MED/DEF** for 12 to 15 minutes. Arrange drained cherries over top of pudding for garnish.

My cooking time:

◄ *Top to bottom Fruit Cream Pudding and Cherry Pie Pudding.*

FRENCH

Egg Custard

TOTAL COOKING TIME: 13 minutes
Serves 4
8-inch round glass baking dish
2-cup glass measuring cup

1½ cups milk
3 eggs
¼ cup sugar
¼ teaspoon salt
1 teaspoon vanilla
Dash nutmeg

In glass measuring cup cook milk on **HIGH** for 3 minutes to scald. In glass baking dish, beat together eggs, sugar, salt, and vanilla. Gradually stir hot milk into egg mixture. Sprinkle with nutmeg. Cook on **MED/DEF** for 9 to 10 minutes or until custard is almost set. Custard will become firm as it cools. Serve chilled.

My cooking time:

Honey-Pumpkin Pudding

TOTAL COOKING TIME: 20 minutes
Serves 8 to 10
2-quart glass mixing bowl

1 can (16-ounces) pumpkin
1½ cups light cream
2 eggs
½ cup honey
½ teaspoon salt
½ teaspoon cinnamon
¼ teaspoon nutmeg
½ cup chopped pecans
Whipped cream

In glass mixing bowl, combine pumpkin, cream, eggs, honey, salt, cinamon, and nutmeg. Cook on **MED/DEF** for 18 to 20 minutes or until thickened, stirring every 4 minutes with wire whip to smooth. Fold in chopped nuts. Serve warm or chilled with whipped cream if desired.

My cooking time:

Chocolate Mousse

TOTAL COOKING TIME: 9 minutes
Serves 12
2-quart glass mixing bowl

2 squares (1-ounce each) baking chocolate
⅔ cup sugar, divided
1 envelope (1 tablespoon) unflavored gelatin
¼ teaspoon salt
3 eggs, separated
1 cup light cream
1 tablespoon rum
1 teaspoon powdered instant coffee
1 cup heavy cream, whipped

In large glass mixing bowl cook chocolate on **HIGH** for 2 to 3 minutes to melt. Stir in ⅓ cup sugar, gelating, salt, egg yolks, and cream. Beat until well blended. Cook on **MED/DEF** for 4 to 6 minutes until thickened. Stir in rum and coffee. Chill. Beat egg whites, gradually add remaining sugar, beating until stiff. Fold egg whites and whipped cream into chilled chocolate mixture. Spoon into individual serving cups. Chill 2 hours.

My cooking time:

Herbed Spinach Bake

TOTAL COOKING TIME: 15 minutes
Serves 6
1½-quart glass baking dish

1 package (10-ounces) frozen chopped spinach, defrosted
1 cup cooked long-grain rice
1 cup shredded processed American cheese
2 eggs slightly beaten
⅓ cup milk
2 tablespoons butter, melted
2 tablespoons chopped onion
1 teaspoon salt
½ teaspoon Worcestershire sauce
¼ teaspoon fines herbes

Drain defrosted spinach well. Combine all ingredients in glass baking dish. Cook on **MED/DEF** for 12 to 15 minutes, stirring twice. Allow to stand 5 minutes to firm.

My cooking time:

◄ *Top to bottom Chocolate Mousse and Honey Pumpkin Pudding.*

Pots de Creme

TOTAL COOKING TIME: 6 minutes
Serves 6
4-cup glass measure

4 egg yolks
1 teaspoon vanilla
¾ cup milk
¾ cup heavy cream
3 squares unsweetened chocolate
½ cup sugar
⅛ teaspoon salt

Beat eggs and vanilla in small mixing bowl until thick and lemon colored. Combine remaining ingredients in glass measuring cup. Cook on **HIGH** for 4 to 6 minutes until chocolate melts and mixture is hot. Do no boil. Blend slowly into egg yolks, beating constantly until smooth. Pour into 6 small serving dishes. Chill. Garnish with whipped cream.

My cooking time: ☐

Potato Cheese Custard

TOTAL COOKING TIME: 13 minutes
Serves 6
1½-quart glass baking dish

1 cup milk
1 jar (5-ounce) processed cheese spread with bacon
1 teaspoon minced onion
2 eggs, beaten
1 tablespoon minced parsley
½ teaspoon salt
½ teaspoon dry mustard
Dash pepper
2 cups diced cooked potatoes
Bacon, crisp-cooked and crumbled

In 2-cup glass measure, mix together milk, cheese spread, and onion. Cook on **HIGH** for 4 minutes, or until cheese melts, stirring occasionally. Meanwhile in 1½-quart glass dish combine eggs, parsley, salt, dry mustard and pepper. Gradually stir hot milk mixture into egg mixture. Cook on **HIGH** for 3 minutes, stirring every ½ minute until thick. Stir in potatoes. Cook on **MED/DEF** for 4 minutes, stir once. Top with bacon; cook on **MED/DEF** for 2 minutes or until firm. Let stand 5 minutes before serving.

My cooking time: ☐

Vanilla Pudding

TOTAL COOKING TIME: 9 minutes
Serves 4
4-cup glass measure

½ cup sugar
⅛ teaspoon salt
2 tablespoons cornstarch
2 cups milk
1 egg, well beaten
1 tablespoon butter
1 teaspoon vanilla

In glass measure combine sugar, salt and cornstarch. Gradually add milk, mixing well. Cook on **HIGH** for 5 to 7 minutes, stirring twice, until mixture is smooth and thick. Add small amount of hot mixture to egg, beating constantly. Add warmed egg mixture to hot pudding, mixing well. Cook on **MED/DEF** for 2 minutes, stirring twice until thickened. Add butter and vanilla. Pour into serving dishes. Chill.

My cooking time: ☐

Tapioca Pudding

TOTAL COOKING TIME: 8 minutes
Serves 6
4-cup glass measure

2 cups milk
2 eggs, separated
⅓ cup sugar
2 tablespoons quick-cooking tapioca
¼ teaspoon salt
1 teaspoon vanilla

In glass measuring cup combine milk, egg yolks, ¼ cup sugar, tapioca, and salt; let stand 5 minutes. Cook on **HIGH** for 6 to 8 minutes or until mixture comes to full boil, stirring frequently. Add vanilla. Beat egg whites until soft peaks form. Gradually, add remaining sugar; beat until sugar disappears. Fold tapioca mixture into egg whites gently but thoroughly. Spoon into serving dishes.

My cooking time: ☐

Pastry & Pies

A flaky, light crust is ready for its filling in just minutes. Crumb crusts of all types are ready in a snap. Making a cool summer pie without heating the kitchen with the conventional oven is as easy as can be with your microwave oven. Even two crust pies can be made faster whether they are scratch or frozen, with the combination of techniques in the chapter.

As a General Rule:

- Always cook uncovered.
- Always use a glass or ceramic pie plate. 9-inch is most desirable.
- If using frozen pie shell, spray pie plate with vegetable oil to prevent crust from sticking to dish.
- Always cook crusts on **HIGH** for fast and flaky results.
- Turn pie at least once during cooking.

Microwave Method: Pastry Shell

Because of the high fat content, pastry items will be a delicate light color when cooked in the microwave oven. Pie shells will be lighter and flakier in texture. Use either a scratch dough, a package mix or frozen dough and cook as recommended below.

1. Arrange crust in 9-inch glass pie dish. If using a frozen pie crust, transfer crust in frozen state from foil pan to a 9-inch glass pie dish.
2. Cook on power level **HIGH** for 1 minute.
3. Prick several times with a fork to keep bubbles from forming.
4. Continue cooking on power level **HIGH** for 1 minute or until brown spots just start to appear.
5. Cool and fill with desired filling.

NOTE: Although you may cook a TV dinner in its original foil pan, you cannot cook a pie crust in its original foil pan. Proper browning and cooking of the crust will not occur because the microwaves can't cook from all sides.

Microwave Method: Two Crust Pie

Prepare your favorite two crust pie recipe and cook as recommended in the double crust pie recipe on page 152.

Microwave Method: Cookie Crumb Crust

Follow the recipe on next page.

Perfect Microwave Pastry

TOTAL COOKING TIME: 6 to 8 minutes
Makes two 9-inch pastry shells
9-inch glass pie plate

2 cups flour
⅔ cup shortening
¼ teaspoon salt
1 tablespoon sugar (optional)
⅓ cup cold water
5 drops yellow food coloring

Blend flour, shortening, salt, and sugar (optional) until mixture is crumbly and in pea-size pieces. Add water and food coloring, and mix until dough comes clean from bowl and forms a ball. Divide dough in half; flatten into 6-inch circles, wrap in plastic wrap and refrigerate for 30 minutes. Roll out pastry ot fit 9-inch pie plate. Flute edge; prick bottom and sides with a fork. Cook on **HIGH** 6 to 8 minutes, or just until brown spots begin to appear.

My cooking time:

For Tart Shells: fit 5-inch rounds of pastry over inverted glass custard cups. Prick well with fork. Cook on **HIGH** for 3 to 3½ minutes. Cool a few minutes; remove from cups. Makes 8 tart shells.

Pastry from a Mix

TOTAL COOKING TIME: 4 to 5 minutes
One 9-inch pastry shell
9-inch glass pie plate

1 stick prepared pie crust mix

Using pie crust stick or mix, prepare as recommended on package for one 9-inch single pastry shell. Roll out and fit into 9-inch glass pie plate. Flute edge; prick bottom and sides with fork. Cook on **HIGH** for 4 to 5 minutes, or just until brown spots begin to appear.

My cooking time:

Frozen Pie Shell

TOTAL COOKING TIME: 4 to 6 minutes
One 9-inch pastry shell
9-inch glass pie plate

1 9-inch frozen pie shell ("deep dish" style works best)

Transfer frozen pie crust from foil pan to glass pie plate. Allow crust to stand at room temperature for 5 minutes to soften. Cook on **HIGH** for 1 minute. Prick bottom and sides of crust. Continue to cook on **HIGH** for 3 to 5 minutes or just until brown spots appear, turn crust once during cooking.

My cooking time:

Cookie Crumb Crusts

TOTAL COOKING TIME: 3 minutes
Makes one 9-inch pie shell
9-inch glass pie plate

⅓ cup butter
1½ cups finely crushed cookie crumbs (vanilla wafers, gingersnaps, chocolate wafers, graham crackers, flake coconut)

In glass pie plate cook butter on **MED/DEF** for 30 seconds or until melted. Stir crumbs into butter until well blended. Press mixture firmly against bottom and sides of pie plate. Cook on **HIGH** for 2 to 2½ minutes.

My cooking time:

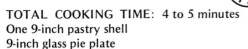

Tangy Lemon Pie

TOTAL COOKING TIME: 5 to 6 minutes
Serves 6 to 8
9-inch glass pie plate

1 9-inch baked pastry shell
1 package (3¼-ounces) lemon pudding and pie filling
¾ cup sugar, divided
¼ cup lemon juice
1¾ cups water
2 eggs, separated
1 teaspoon lemon peel
1 package (3-ounces) cream cheese, cut into chunks
5 drops yellow food coloring, if desired

In a large glass bowl, blend pie filling mix, ½ cup sugar and lemon juice. Stir in water and egg yolks; blend well. Cook on **HIGH** for 5 to 6 minutes, stirring occasionally. Add lemon peel, and cream cheese, stirring until well blended. Add food coloring if desired. Cool mixture until slightly thickened. Beat egg whites until frothy, gradually add remaining ¼ cup sugar. Continue beating until stiff peaks form. Fold into cooled filling. Pour into pastry shell. Chill well before serving. Garnish with lemon slices.

My cooking time:

Lime Delight Pie

TOTAL COOKING TIME: 3 to 4 minutes
Serves 6 to 8
9-inch glass pie plate

1 9-inch chocolate cookie crust
1½ cups water
1 package (3½-ounces) lime gelatin
¼ cup sugar
¼ cup lime juice
2 teaspoons lemon juice
1 carton (4½-ounces) frozen prepared whipped topping, thawed
5 drops green food coloring

In medium glass mixing bowl, bring water to a boil on **HIGH**. Stir in gelatin until dissolved. Chill until partially set. Whip gelatin until fluffy, adding sugar, lime and lemon juices. Fold in whipped topping. Add green food coloring if desired. Chill before serving.

My cooking time:

German Chocolate Pie

TOTAL COOKING TIME: 12 minutes
Serves 8 to 10
9-inch glass pie plate
1-quart glass measuring cup

1 9-inch coconut crust, chilled
1 package (6-ounce) semi-sweet chocolate pieces (1 cup)
1 package (3¼-ounces) chocolate pudding and pie filling mix
2 cups milk
½ cup chopped almonds, toasted
1 cup heavy cream, whipped
Chocolate curls for garnish, if desired

In large custard cup, melt chocolate pieces on **MED/DEF** for 2 to 3 minutes. Spread melted chocolate over chilled coconut crust. Chill. In glass measuring cup, cook pudding mix and milk on **HIGH** for 5 to 6 minutes, stirring occasionally. Add almonds. Cool pudding before pouring into pie shell. Chill pie thoroughly before serving. Top with whipped cream. Garnish with chocolate curls, if desired.

My cooking time:

TIP: To toast nuts in microwave oven, spread ½ cup nuts in pie plate. Cook on **HIGH** for 6 to 8 minutes stirring occasionally until golden.

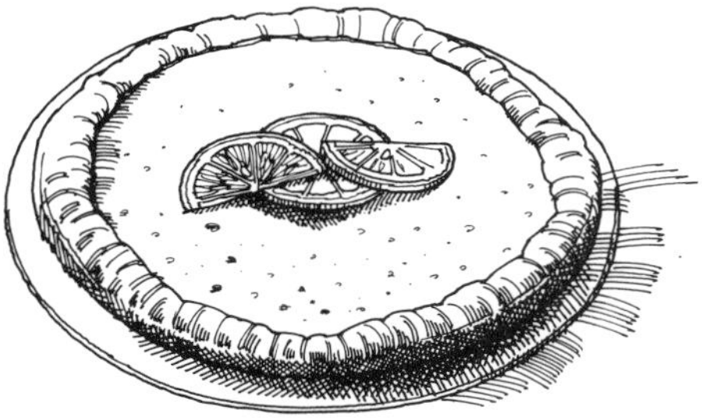

◄ *Tangy Lemon Pie*

Pecan Pie

TOTAL COOKING TIME: 18 to 20 minutes
Serves 6 to 8
9-inch glass pie plate
1-quart glass measuring cup

1 9-inch baked pastry shell
⅓ cup butter
1 cup light corn syrup
3 eggs
1 teaspoon vanilla
¼ teaspoon salt
1 cup packed dark brown sugar
1 cup pecan halves

In a glass measuring cup melt butter on **MED/DEF** for 30 seconds, or until melted. Stir in remaining ingredients mixing well after each addition. Pour into baked pastry shell. Cook on **MED/DEF** for 18 to 20 minutes; turning once during cooking.

My cooking time: ☐

Double Crust Fresh Fruit Pie

TOTAL COOKING TIME: 24 minutes
Serves 6 to 8
9-inch glass pie plate

Preheat conventional oven to 450°F.. Prepare favorite recipe for 2 crust 9-inch fresh fruit pie. Assemble in 9-inch glass pie plate. Seal with fluted edges. With point of sharp knife, cut slits in top crust to allow steam to escape. Cook on **HIGH** for 7 to 8 minutes. Transfer to preheated conventional oven; bake at 450°F for 10 to 15 minutes or until light golden brown.

My cooking time: ☐

TIP: For additional browning on top crust; brush top crust and edges with milk and sprinkle lightly with sugar before cooking .

Pumpkin Pie

TOTAL COOKING TIME: 18 to 20 minutes
Serves 6 to 8
9-inch glass pie plate

1 9-inch baked pastry shell
1 can (16-ounces) canned pumpkin
1 can (14-ounces) sweetened condensed milk
2 eggs
2 teaspoons pumpkin pie spice

Combine pumpkin, sweetened condensed milk, eggs, and spice until blended; pour into shell. Cook on **MED/DEF** for 18 to 20 minutes, turning once while cooking. Center may still appear slightly soft at the end of cooking time. Allow to stand for 30 minutes to firm.

My cooking time: ☐

Cherry Cheese Pie

TOTAL COOKING TIME: 5 minutes
Serves 6 to 8
9-inch glass pie plate

1 9-inch vanilla wafer crumb crust
2 packages (3-ounces each) cream cheese
1 egg
⅓ cup sugar
½ teaspoon almond extract
1 can (21-ounces) cherry pie filling

In a glass mixing bowl, soften cream cheese on **MED/DEF** for 1 minute. Beat cream cheese, egg, sugar, and almond extract until well blended. Spread in bottom of cooled crust. Cook on **MED/DEF** for 3½ to 4 minutes. Cool. Pour cherry pie filling over cheese base. Chill 2 hours before serving.

My cooking time: ☐

Cakes

Microwave baked cakes are easy to prepare and save both preparation and cooking time. The cake texture will be light and airy and the layers will be higher than when cooked conventionally. Whether your favorite cakes are made from scratch or package mixes, you can successfully bake them in your microwave oven.

As a General Rule:

- For best results, bake in round layer, tube or bundt shaped dishes.
- Most layer and oblong cakes bake best when started at a lower power level and finished on high power. (See chart below)
- Tube or Bundt cakes bake well on power level HIGH for entire cooking time.
- Turn dish at least once during baking time to help cook evenly.
- Cook one layer at a time.
- Line dishes with wax paper rather than greasing or flouring. Since bundt pans cannot be lined with wax paper, it may be sprayed with a vegetable oil. (Check instructions packed with bundt dish for best results).
- Test for doneness as you would conventionally. Toothpick when inserted into center of cake should come out clean and edges of cake should start to pull away from sides of dish.
- Cupcakes should be baked in paper cupcake liners in custard cups or cupcake dish designed for microwave use. Fill with 2 tablespoons of batter per cupcake.
- Always place cake on a heatproof flat surface to cool, not on a cake rack. This will help the cake finish cooking evenly. Remove cake from dish after it sets for 5 minutes.

Microwave Method:

Prepare your favorite batter and then bake as follows:

1. Prepare desired cake dish as recommended above.
2. Pour batter into dish, but fill only half full. If overfilled, the batter will run oversides of dish as it cooks.
3. Bake on power level **MED/DEF** for time recommended on Cake Baking Chart and on power level **HIGH** for time recommended on Cake Baking Chart, or until cake tests done. Bake one layer at a time.
4. Let cake cool on heat proof counter for 5 minutes before removing from dish.

My Notes:

CAKE BAKING CHART

Type of Dish	Baking Time Power Level MED/DEF	Baking Time Power Level HIGH
Round 8″ or 9″	6 min.	3 min.
Square 8″ or 9″	6 min.	3 mins.
Tube or Bundt 10 — 12 cup size	12 min.	3 min.
Cupcakes: 1 3 6	 45 to 60 seconds 2 to 3 min. 4 to 5 min.	

TIP: If a cake seems to bake unevenly, try covering it with a piece of wax paper as it cooks.
*Heavy cakes such as carrot cakes will require 2 to 4 minutes additional baking time on power level **HIGH**.

Pineapple Upside-Down Cake

TOTAL COOKING TIME: 12 minutes
Makes 1 layer cake
8-inch round glass baking dish

¼ cup butter
⅓ cup packed brown sugar
¼ cup chopped pecans
1 can (8½-ounces) pineapple slices, drain and reserve juice
Maraschino cherries
1 package (9-ounces) yellow cake mix (1-layer size)

Combine butter, sugar, and nuts in glass baking dish. Cook on **HIGH** for 2 minutes, or until butter and sugar melt to form syrup. Arrange pineapple rings and cherries in syrup. Prepare cake mix according to package directions, substituting reserved pineapple juice for some of the required water. Pour evenly over fruit. Cook on **MED/DEF** for 7 minutes. Rotate dish. Cook on **HIGH** for 3 minutes. Immediately invert onto serving platter and remove dish. Serve warm with whipped cream if desired.

My cooking time:

German Chocolate Cake

TOTAL COOKING TIME: 24 minutes
Makes 2-layer cake
2 8-inch round glass baking dishes

½ cup butter
¼ cup milk
1 package (10-ounces) coconut-pecan frosting mix
1 package (19-ounces) German chocolate cake mix

In medium glass mixing bowl combine butter, milk, and frosting mix. Cook on **HIGH** for 2 minutes until mixture i s bubbly. Stir well; divide evenly between 2 glass baking dishes. Prepare cake mix according to package directions. Pour half of cake batter into each dish. Cook one layer at a time on **MED/DEF** for 7 minutes. Rotate dish and continue to cook on **HIGH** for 3 to 4 minutes. Cool for 5 minutes. Loosen edges. Invert onto serving dish, stacking both layers together with frosted sides up.

My cooking time:

Creamy Apple Cake

TOTAL COOKING TIME: 13 minutes
Serves 6
10 x 6-inch glass baking dish

1 package (9-ounces) yellow cake mix (1-layer size)
¼ cup butter, softened
2 eggs
1 can (20-ounces) sliced apples, drained
1 cup sour cream
TOPPING
1 cup graham cracker crumbs
⅓ cup butter
⅓ cup brown sugar
⅓ cup chopped nuts
1 teaspoon cinnamon
½ teaspoon ground nutmeg

Combine cake mix, butter and one egg, blend well. Spread batter in glass baking dish. Cook on **HIGH** for 3 to 4 minues. Arrange apple slices over base. Blend sour cream and remaining egg, spread evenly over apples. Combine topping ingredients in small glass mixing bowl. Cook on **HIGH** for 1 minute. Stir to blend. Sprinkle topping mixture over sour cream layer. Cook on **MED/DEF** for 8 minutes. Serve warm. Refrigerate leftovers.

My cooking time: ______

Boston Cream Pie

TOTAL COOKING TIME: 19 minutes
Serves 6
8-inch round glass baking dish
1-quart glass measuring cup

1 package (9-ounces) yellow cake mix (1-layer size)
1 package (4-ounces) vanilla pudding and pie filling
CHOCOLATE GLAZE
2 squares unsweetened chocolate
¼ cup butter
3 tablespoons milk
2 cups powdered sugar
⅛ teaspoon salt
½ teaspoon vanilla
Sliced almonds

Prepare cake mix according to package directions. Pour batter into wax paper lined glass baking dish. Cook on **MED/DEF** for 7 minutes. Turn dish ¼ turn. Cook on **HIGH** for 3 minutes. Cool cake for 10 minutes; remove from dish. Prepare pudding mix according to package directions in glass measuring cup. Cook on **HIGH** for 6 minutes, stirring occasionally. Cool. Split cake layer in half to make 2 thin layers. Spread cooled pudding between layers. In medium glass mixing bowl, combine chocolate, butter, and milk. Cook on **HIGH** for 3 minutes or until chocolate melts. Add sugar, salt, and vanilla; blend until smooth. Frost top with glaze, allowing glaze to drip down sides. Garnish with almonds. Refrigerate until serving time.

My cooking time: ______

Black Forest Cake

TOTAL COOKING TIME: 12 to 18 minutes
Serves 10 to 12
2 8-inch glass baking dishes *or* Bundt or tube microwave dish

1 package (19-ounces) chocolate cake mix
2 eggs
¼ cup oil
½ cup water
1 can (22-ounces) cherry pie filling
1 teaspoon almond extract
Sifted powdered sugar

Mix cake mix, eggs, oil, and water until well blended. Stir in pie filling and flavoring.
For 2-layer cake: Divide batter between 2 wax paper lined glass baking dishes, cook one layer at a time on **MED/DEF** for 7 minutes. Turn dish. Cook on **HIGH** for 3 minutes. After 5 minutes; remove cake from dish to cool. Stack layers and dust with powdered sugar before serving.
For bundt or tube cake: Follow dish manufactuer's instructions regarding greasing. Pour batter into dish. Cook on **HIGH** for 10 to 12 minutes. Turn dish every 3 minutes. After 5 minutes, remove cake from dish to cool. Dust with powdered sugar before serving.

My cooking time: ______

◄ *Top to bottom: Boston Cream Pie and Creamy Apple Cake.*

Poppy Seed Cake

TOTAL COOKING TIME: 10 minutes
Serves 8 to 10
2 8-inch glass baking dishes *or* Bundt or tube microwave dish

1 package (19-ounces) yellow cake mix
2 eggs
1 cup water
¼ cup poppy seeds
1 teaspoon almond extract
Sifted powdered sugar

Beat cake mix, eggs, and water for 3 minutes with electric mixer. Add poppy seeds and almond extract; beat until well mixed.
For 2-layer cake: Divide batter between 2 wax paper lined glass baking dishes. Cook one layer at a time on **MED/DEF** for 7 minutes. Rotate dish. Cook on **HIGH** for 3 minutes. After 5 minutes, remove cake from dish to cool. Stack layers and dust with powdered sugar.
For bundt or tube cake: Follow dish manufacturer's instructions regarding greasing. Pour batter into dish. Cook on **HIGH** for 9 to 10 minutes. Turn dish every 3 minutes. After 5 minutes, remove cake from dish to cool. Dust with powdered sugar before serving.

My cooking time:

Carrot Cake

TOTAL COOKING TIME: 12 to 15 minutes
Serves 10 to 12
12 x 7-inch glass baking dish *or* tube or Bundt microwave dish

1½ cups flour
1½ teaspoons baking powder
1¼ teaspoons soda
¾ teaspoon salt
2 teaspoons cinnamon
1½ cups sugar
1 cup oil
3 eggs
2 cups grated carrots
1 can (8¼-ounces) crushed pineapple, drained
½ cup chopped walnuts
Cream Cheese Frosting

Sift flour, baking powder, soda, salt, and cinnamon. Add sugar, oil and eggs and mix well. Stir in carrots, drained pineapple and nuts.
For 12 x 7-inch cake: Pour into greased 12 x 7-inch glass baking dish. Cook on **HIGH** for 14 to 16 minutes, turning after 8 minutes.
For bundt or tube cake: Follow dish manufacturer's instructions regarding greasing. Pour batter into pan. Cook on **HIGH** for 10 to 12 minutes. After 5 minutes, remove cake from pan to cool. Frost cake when cool, if desired.

Cream Cheese Frosting
¼ cup butter
1 package (3-ounces) cream cheese
2 cups powdered sugar
1 teaspoon vanilla

Combine ingredients in glass mixing bowl. Cook on **HIGH** for 30 seconds to soften. Beat until fluffy.

My cooking time:

Blueberry Coffee Cake

TOTAL COOKING TIME: 8 minutes
Serves 6
8-inch round glass baking dish

1 package (13-ounces) blueberry muffin mix
1 teaspoon instant coffee
2 tablespoons sugar
1 teaspoon cinnamon

Prepare muffin mix according to package directions, adding instant coffee to batter. Pour into wax paper lined glass baking dish. Cook on **MED/DEF** for 5 minutes. Rotate dish. Cook on **HIGH** for 2 to 3 minutes. Turn cake out onto serving platter. Sprinkle with mixture of sugar and cinnamon.

My cooking time:

Christmas Plum Pudding

TOTAL COOKING TIME: 15 minutes
Makes 2 plum puddings
1-quart glass measuring cup

1½ cups flour, divided
½ pound suet
2 cups raisins
2 cups chopped dates
3 cups fresh bread crumbs
1 orange
1 lemon
7 tart apples, cored, peeled, and chopped
½ cup ground blanched almonds
1 cup brown sugar
½ teaspoon ground cloves
2 teaspoons cinnamon
1 teaspoon *each* ground ginger, mace, salt
½ cup cognac
6 eggs, beaten slightly
Additional cognac

Chop suet very fine and sprinkle with ½ cup flour. Dust raisins, and dates with flour and add to suet. Add bread crumbs. Grate rinds of orange and lemon, squeeze juice and combine juice and peel with suet mixture. Add remaining flour, apples, nuts, brown sugar, all spices and salt. Mix well, add ½ cup cognac and store in cold place or refrigerator until ready to cook. May be stored for up to two weeks. Each day add ¼ cup cognac to mixture. On last day, stir well and add the eggs.

To cook: Line a 1-quart glass measuring cup with brown paper. Fill with ½ of mixture and cover tightly with plastic wrap. Cook on **HIGH** for 12 to 15 minutes or until done in the center. After it cools, remove from glass cup and wrap well. Store in refrigerator until ready to serve.

To serve: Cook on **HIGH** for 4 to 5 minutes. Heat ¼ cup cognac for 30 seconds. Light the cognac and pour over pudding to flame.

My cooking time: ______

TIP: Wrap cooked puddings in cheesecloth soaked in cognac ' foil for added flavor.

Graham Streusel Cake

TOTAL COOKING TIME: 11 minutes
Serves 6
8-inch round glass baking dish

1 cup graham cracker crumbs
⅓ cup butter
⅓ cup packed brown sugar
⅓ cup chopped nuts
1 teaspoon cinnamon
1 package (9-ounces) yellow cake mix (1-layer size)

GLAZE
1 cup powdered sugar
1 to 2 tablespoons milk

Combine in small glass mixing bowl, graham cracker crumbs, butter, sugar, nuts, and cinnamon. Cook on **HIGH** for 1 minute. Stir to blend. Spread half of topping mixture in wax paper lined glass baking dish. Prepare cake mix according to directions. Pour half of cake batter into dish. Top with remaining topping mixture, then remaining cake batter. Cook on **MED/DEF** for 7 minutes. Rotate dish. Cook on **HIGH** for 3 minutes. Invert onto serving dish. Combine powdered sugar and milk to make glaze. Drizzle with glaze.

My cooking time: ______

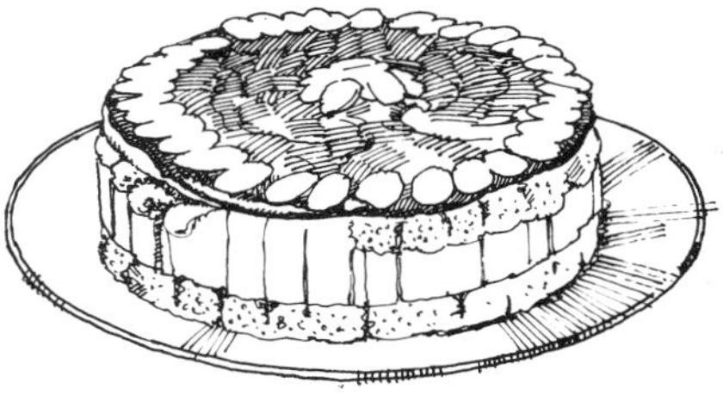

Pumpkin Spice Cake

TOTAL COOKING TIME: 12 to 18 minutes
Serves 10 to 12
2 8-inch glass baking dishes *or* Bundt or tube microwave dish

1 package (19-ounces) spice cake mix
2 eggs
¼ cup oil
½ cup water
1 can (16-ounces) pumpkin
½ cup chopped walnuts
Sifted powdered sugar

Mix cake mix, eggs, oil, water, and pumpkin until well blended. Stir in nuts.

For 2-layer cake: Divide batter between 2 wax paper lined glass baking dishes. Cook one layer at a time on **MED/DEF** for 7 minutes. Turn dish. Cook on **HIGH** for 3 minutes. After 5 minutes, remove cake from dish to cool. Stack layers and dust with powdered sugar before serving.

For bundt or tube cake: Follow dish manufacturer's instructions regarding greasing. Pour batter into dish. Cook on **HIGH** for 10 to 12 minutes. Turn dish every 3 minutes. After 5 minutes, remove cake from dish to cool. Dust with powdered sugar before serving.

My cooking time: ☐

Creme de Menthe Cheesecake

TOTAL COOKING TIME: 15 minutes
Serves 10 to 12
8-inch round glass baking dish

¼ cup butter
1¼ cup chocolate cookie crumbs
4 packages (3-ounces each) cream cheese
½ cup sugar
2 eggs
¼ cup green Creme de Menthe
2 teaspoons white Cream de Cacao
TOPPING
½ cup semi-sweet chocolate pieces
½ cup sour cream, at room temperature

Place butter in glass baking dish. Cook on **HIGH** for 1 minute. Add crumbs, stir until well mixed. Press onto bottom and sides of dish. Cook on **HIGH** for 2 minutes. In large bowl beat cream cheese and sugar until fluffy; add eggs and liqueurs. Beat thoroughly. Pour into crust. Cover with wax paper, cook on **MED/DEF** for 7 to 10 minutes, turning dish after 5 minutes. Cool. Melt chocolate pieces by cooking on **MED/DEF** for 2 minutes. Blend in sour cream. Spread chocolate glaze over surface of cooled pie and refrigerate at least 3 hours before serving.

My cooking time: ☐

Fruit Cocktail Cake

TOTAL COOKING TIME: 18 minutes
Serves 12
2 8-inch round glass baking dishes

2 eggs
⅔ cup sugar
⅔ cup brown sugar
2 cups flour
2 teaspoons baking soda
1 can (16-ounces) fruit cocktail
½ cup finely chopped walnuts
TOPPING
¾ cup sugar
1 can (5⅔-ounce) evaporated milk
1 cup butter
1 teaspoon vanilla
1 cup toasted flaked coconut

With electric mixer combine eggs, sugars, flour, soda and liquid from fruit cocktail. Mix until well blended. On low speed, fold in fruit cocktail and nuts. Divide batter evenly between two round glass dishes. Cook one layer at a time on **MED/DEF** for 6 minutes. Turn dish. Cook on **HIGH** for 3 minutes. Repeat for second layer. Spread topping over hot cake. Serve warm.

TOPPING: In 4-cup glass measure combine milk, sugar and butter. Cook on **HIGH** for 3 minutes or until boiling. Cook on **MED/DEF** for 2 minutes to simmer. Add vanilla and coconut. Spread over hot cake.

My cooking time: ☐

Bar Cookies & Treats

The best type of cookies to make in a microwave oven are bar cookies. So many of us forget that these cookies are easier to make than individual cookies because they require less preparation and cooking time. They become even more of a time and energy saver when done in a microwave oven, so start serving a greater variety of bar cookies. Your familly will be glad you did.

So often the constant stirring or watching that sweets, such as caramel apples, fudge or pralines, require when done conventionally will discourage us from making these fun to serve desserts. When cooked in a microwave oven they truly are fun to make because they only require a minimum of watching. Microwaves heat as delicately as a double boiler, so there is no hot pan to cause scorching.

As a General Rule: Bar Cookies

- Bake in a glass baking dish. Round, oblong or square can be used. Choose an appropriate size for what you are making.
- Cover with wax paper when cooking
- When storing microwave cooked bar cookies, be sure to keep them covered so they stay moist.

As a General Rule: Treats

- Use a dish 2 to 3 times the volume of the recipe to accommodate the boiling mixture.
- Very little stirring will be required.
- Foods with a large amount of sugar heat to a very high temperature. Be sure to use a container which can withstand high temperatures. Be careful when removing from oven.

Microwave Method:

Every recipe in this chapter is a little different so there is no set microwave method. When trying your favorite recipes of this type, we suggest you prepare it using the same instructions as a similar recipe in this chapter.

Chocolate Nut Balls

TOTAL COOKING TIME: 2 minutes
Makes about 40 cookies
Large glass mixing bowl

1 package (6-ounces) semi-sweet chocolate pieces (1 cup)
1 can (5⅓-ounces) evaporated milk
2½ cups crushed vanilla wafers
½ cup powdered sugar
2 tablespoons rum
1⅓ cups finely chopped walnuts, divided

In large glass mixing bowl, place chocolate pieces and milk. Cook on **HIGH** for 2 minutes, or until chocolate melts, stirring after 1 minute. Stir in crushed wafers, sugar, rum and ⅓ cup chopped nuts. Mix until well blended. Let stand at room temperature about 1 hour. Form into small balls with hands and roll in remaining chopped nuts to coat. Store in refrigerator.

My cooking time: ________

Peanut Bars

TOTAL COOKING TIME: 5 to 6 minutes
Makes 20 to 24 bars
10 x 6-inch glass baking dish

1 package (11-ounces) pie crust mix
1 cup firmly packed dark brown sugar
½ cup peanut butter
3 tablespoons water
1 package (6-ounces) semi-sweet chocolate pieces (1 cup)
½ cup chopped peanuts

Combine pie crust mix, brown sugar, peanut butter, and water in large mixing bowl; mix well to combine. Spread and flatten into glass baking dish. Cover with wax paper. Cook on **HIGH** for 5 to 6 minutes until mixture is puffy, but firm. Sprinkle chocolate pieces over top. Cook on **HIGH** for 30 seconds to soften. Spread chocolate to frost bars; top with chopped peanuts. Cool. Cut into bars.

My cooking time: ________

Rocky Road Brownies

TOTAL COOKING TIME: 12 minutes
Makes 18 bars
12 x 7-inch glass baking dish

1 package (22-ounces) brownie mix
3 eggs
⅓ cup water
FROSTING
¼ cup butter
1 package (6-ounces) semi-sweet chocolate pieces (1 cup)
2¼ cups miniature marshmallows
1 cup salted peanuts

Combine brownie mix, eggs, and water. Spread batter in glass baking dish. Cook on **MED/DEF** for 8 minutes. Turn dish. Cook on **HIGH** for 2 to 3 minutes, or until brownies are dry on top. Combine butter and chocolate pieces in glass mixing bowl. Cook on **HIGH** for 1 minute or until melted. Stir in marshmallows and peanuts, blend well. Top brownies with frosting. Allow to cool. Cut into bars.

My cooking time: ________

Marshmallow Crispy Squares

TOTAL COOKING TIME: 2 minutes
Makes 24 squares
12 x 7-inch glass baking dish

4 cups miniature marshmallows
¼ cup butter
5 cups Rice Krispies

Combine marshamallows and butter in large glass mixing bowl. Cook on **HIGH** for 2 minutes, stirring after 1 minute. Stir to blend butter and marshmallows. Stir in cereal until well coated. Spread into buttered baking dish. Cool. Cut into squares.

My cooking time:

Tipsy Marble Bars

TOTAL COOKING TIME: 8 to 10 minutes
Makes 20 to 24 bars
12 x 7-inch glass baking dish

¼ cup rum
½ cup raisins
½ cup butter
1½ cup graham cracker crumbs
1 package (6-ounces) semi-sweet chocolate pieces (1 cup)
1 cup chopped walnuts
1 can (5-ounces) sweetened condensed milk

Combine rum and raisins in small measuring cup. Cook on **HIGH** for 1 minute, or until cup feels warm to the touch Set aside. In glass baking dish cook butter on **HIGH** for 1 minute, or until melted. Sprinkle with graham cracker crumbs; lightly press into bottom of dish. Layer chocolate pieces, raisins and rum, and walnuts. Pour sweetened condensed milk evenly over the top. Cover with wax paper for first half of cooking period. Cook on **HIGH** for 8 to 10 minutes total or until lightly browned. Cool. Cut into bars.

My cooking time:

Apricot Crumble Bars

TOTAL COOKING TIME: 8 minutes
Makes 16 to 20 squares
8-inch square glass baking dish

¾ cup butter
1 cup packed dark brown sugar
1¾ cups flour
1 teaspoon salt
½ teaspoon baking soda
1½ cups quick cooking oats
1 cup apricot jam

In medium size bowl, cream butter and sugar until fluffy. Stir in flour, salt, baking soda, and oats. Combine until well blended. Press ½ of mixture into bottom of buttered baking dish. Cook on **HIGH** for 4 minutes, turning dish after 2 minutes. Spread jam evenly over baked base. Crumble remaining oat mixture over jam and press lightly. Cook on **HIGH** for 4 minutes. Cool and cut into bars.

My cooking time:

Ting-A-Lings

TOTAL COOKING TIME: 1 minute
Makes 24 to 30 pieces
Large glass mixing bowl

1 package (6-ounces) butterscotch or chocolate pieces (1 cup)
½ cup peanut butter
1 can (5½-ounces) chow mein noodles
½ cup salted peanuts

Combine candy pieces and peanut butter in large glass mixing bowl. Cook on **HIGH** for about 1 minute, stirring after 30 seconds, until melted. Stir in chow mein noodles and peanuts. Drop by rounded teaspoons onto wax paper lined cookie sheets. Refrigerate until set. Store in refrigerator.

My cooking time:

Frosted Oatmeal Chews

TOTAL COOKING TIME: 10 minutes
Makes 24 servings
10 x 6-inch glass baking dish

½ cup butter
½ cup honey
2 cups quick cooking oats
1 package (6-ounces) semi-sweet chocolate pieces (1 cup)
½ cup chunky peanut butter

Cream together butter and sugar. Add honey and oats. Press into glass baking dish. Cover with wax paper, cook on **HIGH** for 4 minutes or until top is bubbly. Cool. Place chocolate pieces and peanut butter in a small glass measuring cup. Cook on **HIGH** for 2 minutes; stir until smooth. Spread on top of oatmeal base. Keep in refrigerator. Cut into small squares.

My cooking time: ______

TIP: For ease in cutting squares, allow to stand at room temperature for 20 minutes.

Mint Melt-away Fudge

TOTAL COOKIG TIME: 8 minutes
Makes about 3 pounds
12 x 7-inch glass baking dish
2-quart glass mixing bowl

3 cups sugar
¾ cup butter
1 can($5\frac{1}{3}$-ounces) evaporated milk
1 package (12-ounces) semi-sweet chocolate pieces (2 cups)
1 jar (7-ounces) marshmallow creme
1 teaspoon peppermint extract

In 2-quart glass mixing bowl combine sugar, butter, and evaporated milk. Cook on **HIGH** for 8 minutes, stirring occasionally. Stir in chocolate pieces until melted. Add marshmallow creme and peppermint extract, beating until well blended. Pour into buttered baking dish. Cool at room temperature; cut into squares.

My cooking time: ______

TIP: For easy spooning of marshmallow creme, remove lid and seal from jar; heat on **HIGH** for 30 seconds.

Hawaiian Pralines

TOTAL COOKING TIME: 10 to 12 minutes
Makes about 24
2-quart glass mixing bowl

1 package (3-ounces) butterscotch pudding & pie filling mix
1 cup sugar
½ cup firmly packed brown sugar
1 can ($5\frac{1}{3}$-ounces) evaporated milk
2 tablespoons butter
1½ cups coarsely chopped macadamia nuts

In glass mixing bowl, combine pudding mix, sugars, milk, and butter. Cook on **HIGH** for 8 to 10 minutes, stirring often, until mixture reaches soft ball stage*. Add nuts. Beat for 2 minutes. Quickly drop by tablespoonfuls onto wax paper lined cookie sheet. Let stand until firm.

My cooking time: ______

TIP: *Soft ball stage is reached when small amount of syrup forms a soft ball when dropped into cold water.

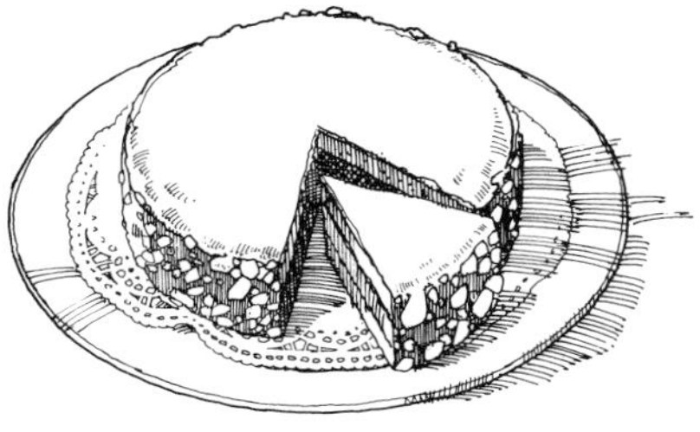

Rocky Road Bon Bons

TOTAL COOKING TIME: 1 to 2 minutes
Makes about 30 pieces
Large custard cup

- 1 package (6-ounces) semi-sweet chocolate pieces (1 cup)
- 30 large marshmallows
- ½ cup toasted, chopped nuts

Place chocolate pieces in custard cup. Cook on **HIGH** for 1½ minutes or until melted and smooth. Dip half of marshmallow into chocolate, then into nuts. Place on wax paper to cool and set.

My cooking time:

TIP: If chocolate begins to harden while dipping, return to oven for a few seconds.

Cinnamon Candy Apples

TOTAL COOKING TIME: 20 minutes
Makes 6 apples
2-quart glass mixing bowl

- 1 cup sugar
- 1 cup light corn syrup
- ½ cup water
- ¼ cup small red cinnamon candies
- ¼ teaspoon red food coloring
- ¼ teaspoon ground cinnamon
- 6 small apples
- 6 wooden sticks

In large glass mixing bowl, combine sugar, corn syrup, water, and candies. Cook on **HIGH** for 10 minutes. Stir to dissolve sugar; add food coloring and cinnamon, mixing thoroughly. Continue to cook on **HIGH** for 8 to 10 minutes, or until mixture reaches crack stage*. While candy is cooking, insert wooden sticks into apples and generously butter cookie sheet. Dip apples quickly into syrup, tipping to coat. Place on buttered cookie sheet to cool.

My cooking time:

NOTE: *Crack stage is reached when syrup dropped in cold water separates into threads which are hard and brittle.

Caramel Apples

TOTAL COOKING TIME: 2 to 3 minutes
Makes 6 apples
1-quart glass mixing bowl

- 1 package (14-ounces) caramel candy
- 2 teaspoons water
- 6 small apples
- 6 wooden sticks
- Toasted nuts, if desired

Place unwrapped candies and water in deep glass bowl. Cook on **HIGH** for 1½ to 2 minutes or until melted, stirring after each minute. Insert sticks into apples. Dip into hot melted caramel, turning to coat. Place on buttered wax paper to cool. If desired sprinkle paper first with toasted chopped nuts.

My cooking time:

Frozen Bananas

TOTAL COOKING TIME: 1½ minutes
Makes 12 pieces
9-inch glass pie dish

- 6 firm bananas
- 1 package (12-ounces) semi-sweet chocolate pieces (2 cups)
- ⅓ cup butter or creamy peanut butter
- 1 cup chopped toasted nuts
- 12 wooden sticks

Peel and cut bananas crosswise. Insert stick into cut end. Place on cookie sheet in freezer at least 30 minutes before dipping. Combine chocolate and butter in glass pie dish, cook on **HIGH** for 1½ minutes or until melted and smooth. Dip bananas in chocolate mixture and roll in chopped nuts. Return to freezer to firm. Store in plastic bag.

My cooking time:

Getting the Most Out of Your Microwave Oven

Defrosting, Reheating & Convenience Charts

Getting the Most Out of Your Microwave Oven

Convenience, flavor, time and energy savings are all made evident when using the microwave oven as the main cooking appliance in your kitchen. However, there are times when a flavor or brownness is desired which cannot be accomplished in the microwave oven. For this reason, we have added this chapter to further explain the wonders of your microwave oven when used in combination with the other appliances in your kitchen. Through this type of cooking, the results are more colorful, more flavorful and achieved more quickly than when done in one appliance only. Use your imagination to further explore this form of combining cooking techniques. You'll soon find the microwave oven becoming a basic part of your food preparation.

Microwave Oven: Conventional Oven

Perfect results are achieved with the speed of the microwave oven and the browning ability of the conventional oven. Remember that most foods brown beautifully, but in the few food catagories where extra browning is desired, the conventional oven can be a big help.

NOTE: It is faster to brown foods in a conventional oven than with a browning element in the top of a microwave oven.

Examples:
- Cook a casserole in the microwave oven, then broil a few minutes conventionally for a crisp top.
- Heat frozen fish sticks or fillets in microwave oven then broil for a few minutes conventionally for crispness.
- Cook a frozen pie after placing it in a glass pie dish in the microwave oven until the crust is done and the juice bubbles out the slits in the top. Then place it in a hot oven for a few minutes until it is browned to perfection.

Results: In every example listed above, the food had a better flavor, texture and was more moist than when done totally in the conventional oven.

Microwave Oven: Conventional Surface Unit

Some foods cook so quickly in the microwave oven that the natural carmelization of the fats and sugars doesn't have time to develop the brown coloring we are used to. Use your conventional surface unit to achieve the desired brownness.

Examples: We suggest you use a dish which is suitable for both surface unit direct heat and the microwave oven for the following suggestions.

- Steaks: Browned before cooking in the microwave oven will have the desired seared appearance.
- Chicken Parts: Brown as called for in so many recipes before adding the sauce.
- Pork or Lamb Chops: Brown and then quickly finished in the microwave oven.

Results: A Dish which has the seared brown appearance but the juicy flavor achieved by microwave cooking.

Microwave Oven: Barbecue

A microwave oven can really help here. While the coals are heating, the food can be partially cooked in the microwave oven then finished on the grill. Or try some of the other suggestions given below.

Examples:
- While the coals are still hot, sear some extra hamburger patties and then freeze for later cooking in the microwave oven.
- Sear the outside of a frozen roast on the hot coals, then let it thaw in the refrigerator overnight to be cooked in the microwave oven for tomorrow night's dinner.
- Partially cook chicken pieces in the microwave oven while the coals heat then finish them off on the barbecue. Barbecued chicken in half the time.
- If you are barbecuing something and it is not done on time, simply put it in the microwave oven to finish it quickly.

Results: The speed of the microwave oven with the flavor of the barbecue. The meat will be more juicy too!

Microwave Oven: Toaster

Even a toaster can be a help to do joint tasks with the microwave oven. Toast bread then place cheese slices between and heat in the microwave oven; toasted cheese sandwiches in half a minute without a dirty pan.

Microwave Oven: Freezer

When preparing foods such as soups, chili, spaghetti sauce, etc., make a double recipe. Freeze the other portion and then reheat it later when you need a meal extra fast.

Result: SAVES TIME!!!!!

Microwave Oven: Food Preparation

Think of the many ways your microwave oven can save you work in the kitchen.

Examples:
- Mashed Potatoes: Cook the potatoes in the electric mixer bowl – provided it is glass – and then simply mash and serve.
- Hash Browns: Grate and par cook the potatoes in the microwave oven until tender, then simply brown conventionally and serve.
- Potato Salad: Cook the potatoes in their skins in the microwave oven, then peel, dice and mix. No dirty pans to wash.
- Par cook any vegetables before putting them in casseroles or other ingredients to cut down on the total cooking time.
- Cook puddings or sauces right in the bowl and then place it in the refrigerator.

Results: Less time spent on dirty dishes or preparing a food for serving. That's a good result any time.

Meal Planning

Now that you know the basics of microwave energy cooking, you'll want to cook entire meals in your new Toshiba Microwave Oven. The trick is preparing the food so that everything is ready to serve at the same time. The following steps will show you how:

1. Read each recipe to ensure you understand it and have the necessary ingredients and utensils available and close at hand.
2. Do any pre-preparation such as; chopping, grating or peeling beforehand.
3. Have each recipe ready to enter the oven before you begin cooking. You can set the table as the meal cooks.
4. Use time in the morning to prepare part of the dinner, then simply reheat it at dinner time.

The proper cooking order is determined by the heat retaining quality of the foods being prepared. Foods that retain heat the longest should be cooked first and are listed in Group 1.Because of "standing time" these foods should remain hot while group 2 and 3 are cooking.

NOTE: If Group 1 or 2 should cool before serving time, reheat for a few minutes while you are calling everyone to the table. Group 3 should always be heated just before it goes to the table.

GROUP 1 Meats, Baked Potatoes, Casseroles
GROUP 2 Ground Meats, Fish, Vegetables, Sauces, Gravy
GROUP 3 Breads and Rolls, reheating only
GROUP 4 Desserts, reheating only

Here is a sample menu listed in the order that it is cooked in the microwave oven:
1. Meat Loaf
2. Baked Potatoes
3. Green Beans
4. Rolls
5. Cherry Pie (reheating to serve)

It is a good idea to make dessert early in the day or before the rest of the meal and then simply reheat it while dinner is being eaten.

My Notes:

Defrosting, Reheating & Convenience Charts

Defrosting Chart: Defrost Setting

Use the chart below for defrosting foods in this microwave oven. Refer back to the introductory part of the cookbook for full defrosting instructions, if necessary.

Remember that all times are approximate because freezer temperatures vary. Add a few more minutes of defrosting time, **after the standing time** if necessary.

ITEM	QUANTITY	POWER LEVEL	DEF. TIME	STANDING TIME
BEEF				
Ground	1 lb.	DEFROST	5 minutes	5 minutes
	3 lbs.		12 minutes	5 minutes
Steak	1½ lbs.	DEFROST	10 minutes	10 minutes
Cubed Steak	1 lb.	DEFROST	8 minutes	5 minutes
Rolled Rib Roast	3 lbs.	DEFROST	15 minutes	10 minutes
Chuck Roast	3 lbs.	DEFROST	15 minutes	10 minutes
Stew Meat	1½ lbs.	DEFROST	10 minutes	5 minutes
Hamburger Pattie	1 pc. 4 oz.	DEFROST	2 minutes	3 minutes
Rolled Roast	5 lbs.	DEFROST	25 minutes	15 minutes
Roast Bone-in	5 lbs.	DEFROST	22 minutes	15 minutes
Roast-Chuck, 7-Bone Round Bone	5 lbs.	DEFROST	22 minutes	10 minutes
Ground	5 lbs.	DEFROST	15 minutes	10 minutes
PORK				
Pork Chops 5 oz. each	4 pcs.	DEFROST	10 minutes	5 minutes
Spareribs	1½ lbs.	DEFROST	10 minutes	5 minutes
	3 lbs.	DEFROST	18 minutes	10 minutes
Tenderloin	2 lbs.	DEFROST	10 minutes	5 minutes
Roast	3 lbs.	DEFROST	15 minutes	10 minutes
Roast Rolled	5 lbs.	DEFROST	25 minutes	15 minutes
Roast—Bone-in	5 lbs.	DEFROST	25 minutes	15 minutes

ITEM	QUANTITY	POWER LEVEL	DEF. TIME	STANDING TIME
VEAL				
Ground	1 lb.	DEFROST	5 minutes	5 minutes
Chops	1 lb.	DEFROST	10 minutes	5 minutes
POULTRY				
Chicken Breast	2 lbs.	DEFROST	10 minutes	5 minutes
	3 lbs.			
Drumsticks	1 lb.	DEFROST	10 minutes	5 minutes
Wings	1½ lbs.	DEFROST	8 minutes	5 minutes
Thighs	1 lb.	DEFROST	10 minutes	5 minutes
Roasting Chicken	5 lbs.	DEFROST	20 minutes	10 minutes
Turkey	12 lbs.	DEFROST	40 minutes	20 minutes
Chicken Fryer (Cut-up)	3 lbs.	DEFROST	14–16 min.	5 minutes
FISH & SEAFOOD				
Fish Fillet	1 lb.	DEFROST	5 minutes	—
Whole Fish	1½ lbs.	DEFROST	8 minutes	—
Lobster Tail	8 oz.	DEFROST	2 minutes	5 minutes
Scallops	1 lb.	DEFROST	5 minutes	5 minutes
BREAD	1 loaf	DEFROST	3 minutes	5 minutes
	1 slice	DEFROST	30 seconds	1 minute
ROLLS				
Dinner	4	DEFROST	1½ minutes	1 minute
Sweet	2	DEFROST	1 minute	1 minute
CAKE				
Iced	1 layer	DEFROST	2 minutes	5 minutes
	1 layer	DEFROST	3 minutes	5 minutes

Reheating Chart

Use the charts below for reheating foods taken either from the refrigerator or freezer. If using the food probe to heat to a desired internal temperature, insert the probe into the middle of the food item. When possible, cover with plastic wrap. This will help the food to heat faster and more evenly. The probe will easily go through the plastic wrap.

ITEM	QUANTITY	COOKING TIME	INTERNAL TEMP.	POWER LEVEL
Casserole	1 cup	2½ min.	150°F	HIGH
Lasagna	1 serving	4 min.	150°F	HIGH
Spaghetti Sauce	2 cups	4½ min.	160°F	HIGH
Beef Stroganoff	2 cups	3½ min.	150°F	HIGH
Mashed Potatoes	1 cup	2½ min.	150°F	HIGH
Chicken	3 pieces	4 min.	150°F	HIGH
Sliced Roast	3 slices	1 min.	150°F	HIGH
Fish Fillet	1 serving	1 min.	150°F	HIGH
Baby Food	1 jar	45 sec.	150°F	HIGH
Soup	1 bowl	3 min.	160°F	HIGH
Canned Food	2 cups	4 min.	160°F	HIGH

REHEATING STORAGE TIPS

- For later reheating, refrigerate foods in refrigerator-to-oven safe dishes. This will eliminate extra washing. Check dish manufacturer's instructions as to whether or not the dish can safely go from refrigerator to oven.
- To eliminate the burden of breaking off serving portions of frozen food, freeze in individual serving amounts.
- If the members of your family all run on different schedules, a great asset would be an item such as a SEAL-A-MEAL™ in which foods are sealed in heat proof bags. This way foods can be frozen in individual portions and after piercing bag, can be popped

right into the Microwave Oven and cooked in the bag at the convience of each family member.

- When freezing large quantities of food, freeze in dish it will later be reheated in. When frozen, transfer to plastic bag. When you are ready to reheat, remove from bag and food will fit right into reheating dish.
- Freeze chopped onions in ice cube trays. Each square is about 1 tablespoon. These can easily be thawed in your Microwave Oven for use in casseroles, sauces, soups, etc.

Reheating Chart: Frozen Foods

Because frozen foods are more dense it takes longer for the microwaves to penetrate. Thus, to eliminate outer food from becoming overdone, stirring the food is recommended as it thaws and starts to heat.

ITEM	QUANTITY	COOKING TIME	POWER LEVEL
Casserole	1 cup	5 minutes	HIGH
Lasagna	1 serving	7 minutes	HIGH
Spaghetti Sauce	2 cups	6 minutes	HIGH
Beef Stroganoff	2 cups	6 minutes	HIGH
Mashed Potatoes	1 cup	3 minutes	HIGH
Chicken	3 pieces	5 minutes	HIGH
Sliced Roast	3 slices	2½ minutes	HIGH
Fish Fillets	1 serving	2 minutes	HIGH

NOTE: As with the defrosting charts, the above times are approximate. The starting temperature of the food will determine how quickly it reheats. More or less time should be used accordingly. The above times are for foods just taken either from the refrigerator or freezer.

Convenience Foods

The microwave Oven can be used to prepare many ready-made, convenience frozen foods. In some cases, the foil container can be placed in the oven, but in most cases the results are better if the food is placed in a microwave-safe dish. For example, TV dinner foil trays that are very shallow and reasonably full of food can be placed directly in the oven. When placing the foil trays in the oven, remove any foil covering and return the tray to the box. Heat the tray in the box to help hold the heat in. Be careful that no part of the tray touches the walls of the oven. There are some frozen main dishes available in deep foil trays (about 1 inch.) These foods should be removed from their containers before they are placed in the oven, and stirred frequently for more even heating.

"Dry" frozen appetizers such as pizza or baked potatoes should be heated on several thicknesses of paper towels.

Cakes and sweet rolls can be heated right on serving plates. Keep them in the oven just until warm or they will tend to be dry when cool.

The heating time for foods will depend on the temperature of the food when it is put into the oven. The heating time for frozen foods will vary according to the degree to which the food has thawed out before heating. The time also varies by type of food. Check our tip section of the chart to help achieve the desired cooking results with each type of food.

The following chart is designed to be a quick reference Guide. We have grouped as many items together as possible so look for a type of food, such as frozen vegetables and size of package for proper heating times.

Convenience Heating Chart

ITEM	QUANTITY	POWER LEVEL	COOKING TIME	TIPS
Frozen Vegetables	8–10 oz. Pkg.	HIGH	5–6 minutes	May be cooked in pkg. or covered dish
Frozen Corn on the Cob	4 ears	HIGH	10 minutes	
Frozen Appetizers	6 oz Pkg.	HIGH	2 minutes	Heat on paper towels
Frozen Main Dishes				
Pasta & Sauce	8 oz. Pkg.	HIGH	8 minutes	Heat in glass dish
	20 oz. Pkg.		15 minutes	
Meat Entree	8–10 oz. Pkg.	HIGH	5 minutes	
	15–17 oz. Pkg.	HIGH	10 minutes	
Cook-in Bag	5 oz.	HIGH	10 minutes	Cook right in bag. Pierce bag.
Fried Chicken	32 oz. Pkg.	HIGH	10 minutes	Heat on paper towels
Pizza	24–26½ oz. Pkg.	HIGH	10 minutes	Heat on paper towels
Frozen Dinners				
Large Size	18½ oz.	HIGH	*8 minutes	*Heat on plate & cover with plastic wrap for best result
Reg. Size	10–12 oz.	HIGH	*5 minutes	*If heated in metal tray add 2 minutes.
Frozen Breakfast Foods				
Jelly Donuts	6 oz.	HIGH	3 minutes	Heat on paper towel
French Toast	6 slices	HIGH	3 minutes	
Pancakes	6	HIGH	3 minutes	

Cookbook Index

A

B

D

E

F

P

Q

R

S

T

V

W

Y

Z

Weight & Measure Charts

Mass Kitchen Measurements:

16 ounces (oz.) = 1 pound (lb.)
1000 grams (g) = 1 kilogram (kg)
1 gram (g) = 0.035 ounces
1 kilogram = 2.204 pounds

1 drop = 1/100 teaspoon = 0.05 ml
1 teaspoon = 1/6 fl. oz. = 4.74 ml
1 teaspoon (used in Canadian hospitals) = 5 ml
1 tablespoon (used in Canadian hospitals) = 15 ml

1 Cup = 8 fl. oz. approx. = 227 ml approx.
1 Milk bottle = 1 pt. approx. = 568 ml approx.
1 Wine bottle = 26 fl. oz. approx. = 739 ml approx.

Ounces and Pounds to Grams and Kilograms

Ounces	g	Pounds	kg
1	28.35	1	0.4536
2	56.70	2	0.9072
3	85.05	3	1.3608
4	113.40	4	1.8144
5	141.75	5	2.2680
6	170.10	6	2.7216
7	198.45	7	3.1751
8	226.80	8	3.6287
9	255.15	9	4.0823
10	283.50	10	4.5359
11	311.84		
12	340.19		
13	368.54		
14	396.89		
15	425.24		
16	453.59		

16 ounces (oz.) = 1 pound (lb.)
1000 grams (g) = 1 kilogram (kg)
1 pound = 0.453 592 37 kg exactly.

Useful Temperatures:

Water Freezing point 0.0°C = +32.0°F
Water Boiling point 100.0°C = 212.0°F

Grams/Kilograms to Pounds/Ounces

g	Ounces	g	* lb.	oz.
1	0.0353	100		3.53
2	0.0706	200		7.06
3	0.1059	300		10.59
4	0.1412	400		14.12
5	0.1765	500	1	1.65
6	0.2118	600	1	5.18
7	0.2471	700	1	8.21
8	0.2824	800	1	12.24
9	0.3179	900	1	15.77
10	0.3530	1000	2	3.3
		kg	*** lb.**	**oz.**
10	0.353	1	2	3.3
20	0.706	2	4	6.6
30	1.059	3	6	9.9
40	1.412	4	8	13.1
50	1.765	5	11	0.4
60	2.118	6	13	3.6
70	2.471	7	15	6.9
80	2.824	8	17	10.2
90	3.179	9	19	13.5
100	3.530	10	22	0.7

16 ounces (oz.) = 1 pound (lb.)
1000 grams (g) = 1 kilogram (kg)
1 gram (g) = 0.035 273 962 ounces

* **TO READ TABLES:**
(example) 700 g = 1 lb., 8.21 oz.
and 4 kg = 8 lb., 13.1 oz.

CENTIGRADE TO FAHRENHEIT AND FAHRENHEIT TO CENTIGRADE DEGREES

DEGREES FAHRENHEIT

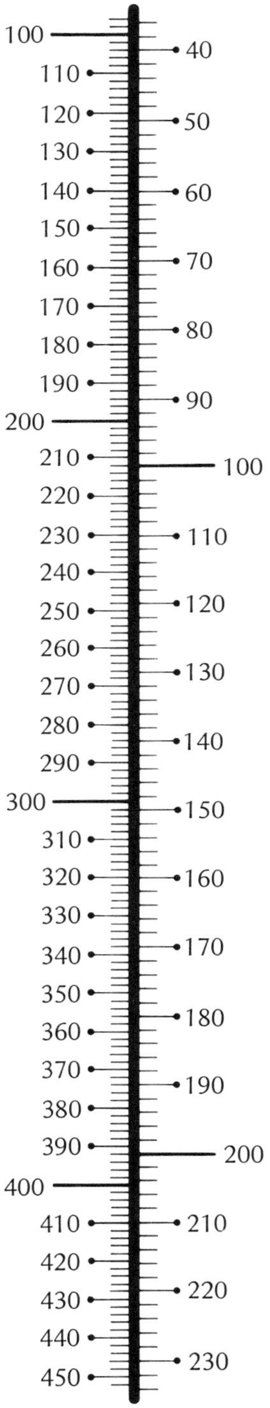

DEGREES CENTIGRADE

CONVERTING TO AND FROM METRIC MEASUREMENTS

Since Metric Measure is becoming more and more important in our daily lives, you will probably want to know how to convert to and from the Metric system easily.
A recipe may require 250 millilitres of milk, while a pint and ounces measuring cup may be all you have available. But if we know a measurement in British (sometimes called Imperial) units, we can always convert to Metric and vice versa, without special equipment. Basically, a Metric measure means a 5% increase over most quantities.

For instance: 250 ml is approximately equal to an 8 oz. cup plus 1 tablespoon
15 ml is approximately equal to 1 tablespoon
5 ml is approximately equal to 1 teaspoon
1 litre is approximately equal to 34 fluid ounces.

But it is always best to be exact. And best to have dual measuring cups and spoons if you can.
We have put together the following conversion scales and charts. You will find them accurate enough for all your microwave cooking purposes.

WEIGHTS, MEASURES, MASS AND TEMPERATURES.

Fluid Measurements:

AMERICAN	BRITISH	METRIC
1 Fluid Ounce	= 1.040 8 fl. oz.	= 29.574 ml
1 Pint	= 0.832 7 pt. (16.65 fl. oz.)	= 473.18 ml
1 Gallon	= 0.832 7 gal. (6 pt. 13 fl. oz.)	= 3.785 4 l

Other Measurements:

AMERICAN	BRITISH	METRIC
1 Bushel (dry)	= 0.968 9 bushel	= 35.238 l
1 Hundredweight (short)	= 100 lb.	= 45.36 kg